Patrick Kennedy

The Fireside Stories of Ireland

Patrick Kennedy

The Fireside Stories of Ireland

ISBN/EAN: 9783337004996

Printed in Europe, USA, Canada, Australia, Japan

Cover: Foto ©Thomas Meinert / pixelio.de

More available books at **www.hansebooks.com**

FIRESIDE STORIES OF IRELAND.

THE FIRESIDE STORIES

OF

IRELAND.

BY
PATRICK KENNEDY,
Author of "Legends of Mount Leinster," "Legends of the
Celts," "The Banks of the Boro," and "Evenings ..."

DUBLIN:
M'GLASHAN AND GILL; AND PATRICK KENNEDY.
LONDON:
SIMPKIN, MARSHALL & CO.; AND BURNS, OATES & CO.;
EDINBURGH; JOHN MENZIES & CO.

1870.

PRINTED BY R. D. WEBB AND SON,
74, MIDDLE ABBEY-STREET.

TO

EDWARD BARRINGTON, ESQ., J.P.,
Fassaroe, Bray.

Dear Sir,

I venture to dedicate to you this little volume, without permission indeed, for I was doubtful of obtaining it if formally asked. I have no other means at command of expressing my gratitude for nearly forty years of uninterrupted and active kindness on your part. I would very willingly bear testimony to your worth as a merchant and a landed proprietor, and to the amount of public good you have done by many beneficent acts, and by furnishing employment to so many hundreds of industrious families during your lifetime ; but, since the days of John Dryden, the language of dedications, however sincere, is not received with undoubted trust. With best wishes for your well-being here and hereafter,

I am,

Dear Sir,

Your faithful servant and friend,

PATRICK KENNEDY.

Dublin, November, 1870.

PREFACE.

A MORE correct title for the present collection would be "The Fireside Stories of the Aryan peoples, as related in Ireland," for nearly every one of them is told in some shape at the social gatherings of Hindoos, Persians, Slavonians, or Teutons. Their skilful framework and the rapid succession of their incidents may in fact account for their popularity, which has endured from a period ages before the commencement of the Christian era. They enjoy a vitality unknown to fictions invented within historic times.

Country folk of the small-farmer and peasant class resort to their neighbours' houses during the long winter evenings, urged by the same want which sends the shopkeepers and mechanics of a city to the reading or tap-room, or the theatre. They soon exhaust the local topics, but are unwilling to withdraw to the comparative loneliness of their own homes; and if one of the company possesses the faculties of a good memory and a good utterance, and condescends to tell a story, he or she is a social benefactor for the time. In this way the great body of fireside lore has been preserved, notwithstanding the small number of good story-tellers in any neighbourhood. Where the office devolves on an incompetent narrator, a change for the worse ensues. Having gone on correctly for a time, he finds his memory at fault, and is obliged to fall back on the sequel of a remembered tale. In this way stories, once popular in this or that locality, come to be remembered no more.

Taking into account the fewness of story-tellers, and the odds against a regular succession of good ones in any given district, the preservation of so many household fictions is not easily accounted for, especially as they have lost the poetic form in which they could be easily retained in the memory. The easy access to cheap books, and the diffusion of the penny literature of our times, have given a death-blow to the oral literature of the fireside. Regret at the passing away of an institution from which my childhood and boyhood derived such pleasure, has set me on to preserve in print the naïve, and in many cases, excellent narratives which once delighted the unlettered folk of half the world. I have endeavoured to present them in a form suitable for the perusal of both sexes and of all ages. Some ludicrous objurgations of no great harm occur, indeed, in some places; for the narrative, as given by a Wexford or Kerry man of the people, would be destitute of local colour without them.

I have only hinted, as it were, at the ordinary pronunciation, giving the words at times as the story-tellers uttered them, and in the correct form at others. A matter-of-fact reader may, if it gives him any pleasure, suppose beast to be always pronounced *baste*, though that faulty *spell* may be used only in a few instances. He must also bring himself to forgive Irish idioms and incorrect orthography in the colloquial parts of a story, while the mere narrative accords tolerably well with rules laid down in Lindley Murray's grammar. This is an ordinary feature of oral recitation. An intelligent though unlettered Bantry or Duffrey peasant or peasantess would recite the troubles of the heroine, the labours and travels of the hero, the evil deeds of giant, giantess, and stepmother in tolerably correct language; but the moment the narrative merged into the colloquial, the native idiom and pronunciation took the upper hand. *Had*, as an auxiliary in the pluperfect tense, will not be met here, as it is not patronised by the Irish people.

Writers born in Hants, or Notts, or Herts will kindly receive a hint or two which may be of use to them, when they venture on the pronunciation of natives of Ireland. Neither Paddy nor Winny ever pronounces Peter *Pather*, nor priest *praste*, nor thief *thafe*, nor read *rade*. He or she will certainly sound beat as if it was spelled *bate*, but neither will ever make a mistake about a word in which occurs either of the diphthongs *ie, ee*. They simply abuse *ea*, and indulge in aspirations—faults which are owing to their retaining the pronunciation of the native Gaelic after the meanings of most of its words have escaped their memory. The diphthong *ea* is never pronounced in Irish as it is heard in *meat*. It is sounded sometimes as *ay* in *day*, and sometimes as *a* in *calf*.

I intended that the present volume should contain some Ossianic and saintly legends, and short historic romances from our ancient annals; but circumstances in which I cannot expect my readers to take any interest have altered the design. These pieces only wait a favourable season to make their appearance. "The Legendary Fictions of the Irish Celts" (Macmillan, 1866), the present, and the projected volume will complete "The Fireside and Bardic Stories of Ireland."

The greater number of the stories appeared in the DUBLIN UNIVERSITY MAGAZINE, while that periodical was the property of Joseph Sheridan Le Fanu, Esq., and while it was enriched by the publication of his best novels. To him and the present proprietor I beg to express my grateful sense of their kind permission to issue a separate edition.

I hope the present collection may give pleasure to many a young and unsophisticated reader, and revive healthy and pleasant recollections of early life in the hearts and minds of those advanced in years.

November, 1870.

CONTENTS.

	Page.
Dedication	v.
Preface	vii.
Hairy Rouchy	3
A Legend of Clever Women	9
The Twelve Wild Geese	14
The Wonderful Cake	19
The False Bride	21
The End of the World	25
The Three Gifts	25
The Unlucky Messenger	30
The Maid in the Country Underground	33
Jack the Cunning Thief	38
The Greek Princess and the Young Gardener	47
The Giant and his Royal Servants	56
The Lazy Beauty and her Aunts	63
The Gilla na Gruaga Donna	67
Shan an Omadhawn and his Master	74
The Princess in the Cat-skins	81
The Well at the World's End	87
The Poor Girl that became a Queen	91
The Grateful Beasts	95
The Gilla Rua	98
The Fellow in the Goat-skin	103
The Haughty Princess	114
Doctor Cure-all	116
The Wise Men of Gotham	119
The Good Boy and the Boy that envied him	122
Choosing the least of Three Evils	125
The Hermit and the Robber	126

Birth and Baptism of St. Mogue	127
The Greedy Mason	128
The Music of Heaven	129
How Donn Firinne got his Horse shod	131
Cliona of Munster	133
A Bullock Changeling	136
How John Hackett won the French Princess	137
The Fairy-stricken Servant	139
The Fairy Rath of Clonnagowan	141
The Fairies' Pass	142
The Banshee of the O'Briens	143
Tom Kiernan's Visit to France	144
The Love Philtre	145
The Pooka of Baltracy	147
The Enchanted Cat of Bantry	149
How the Devil's Glen got its Name	150
The Rock of Cashel	153
The Tree of the Seven Thorns	154
Legend of the Lover's Leap in the Dargle	155
The Discovery of Mitchelstown Caves	156
Lord Clancarty's Ghost	157
The Treasure-seekers of Maynooth	158
The Origin of Loch Erne	160
The Death of the Red Earl	160
Notes and Illustrations	163
Glossary	174

THE FIRESIDE STORIES OF IRELAND.

INTRODUCTION.

There are few literary subjects more obscure in some respects than that of genuine Household Stories. It is acknowledged on all hands that the oral fictions of all the peoples, from Hindoostan to the Hebrides, have had a common origin somewhere in pagan and pre-historic times. But the early recitals of any people did not consist of fictions. They were accounts of past transactions, chiefly the exploits of the ancestors of personages among the auditory of the reciter, and delivered in a poetic form. These in time began to be embellished and enlarged by succeeding bards and minstrels, and, still later, portions of the poetical form escaped the memory of the reciters, and the narratives assumed a prose form. It is vain in our time to seek to recover the original shape of our fireside narratives. Through many transmissions a change for the worse has ensued, and it is beyond the power of our best scholars to determine what ante-historical occurrence or what pagan myth is concealed under the garb of a fireside tale.

Beings of superhuman power, both in human and bestial forms, abound, some good and others evil in their nature, thus testifying to the worship of inferior divinities and of animals.

Morality was not an essential feature of the original narratives, but it is as curious as agreeable to mark the trifling extent of the evil element throughout. Perhaps some improvement was effected in the tales as they passed from the pagan to the christian story tellers. Some indeed of an unedifying character have remained even to our own times, but such as these will not be found in our collection.

Step-mothers and step-sisters were selected by the fireside historians as the antagonistic characters in their compositions. When these were not sufficient for the quota of evil necessary, they added a giant, and occasionally his wife. But in nearly every other instance the mass of shade was subservient to that of the light and the cheerful middle tints of the picture. The good and amiable characters were ever victorious over the selfish and ill-conditioned ones. Our modern social chroniclers adopt the opposite principle. They can only afford such a modicum of light as will give an idea of the depth of their shadows.

Scenes of blood and and cruelty were not at all unfrequent in the ancient repertory, but when it is considered that they were first told to audiences to whom clan-battles, cattle-lifting forays, and all the troubles incident to tribes at variance with their neighbours were things of common occurrence, we may well wonder and be thankful that so many unobjectionable stories were bequeathed by our turbulent ancestors to us their unimaginative and ease-loving descendants.

We flatter ourselves that the stories which we here produce, and which have survived all the changes and chances met in their passage through the countries and the centuries they must have traversed before they reached us, are among the best in the Aryan repertory of fiction. Such as they are, they may be received by our readers as obtained from *bona fide* oral sources. No changes have been made in them by us except where decency required, and they are given in as near an approach to the garb as well as the spirit of the originals as could be furnished by one to the manner born, and to whom, when young, fireside stories were as necessary as daily food and the healthy air from the neighbouring hills. None will more rejoice than he, to hear of some one gathering from a fertile district where the native tongue is still spoken, a harvest of stories racy of the Gaelic idiom, thus accomplishing effectually what he has himself attempted in the comparatively barren field of a semi-English county.

HAIRY ROUCHY.

THERE was once a widow woman, as often there was, and she had three daughters. The eldest and the second eldest were as handsome as the moon and the evening star, but the youngest was all covered with hair, and her face was as brown as a berry, and they called her Hairy Rouchy. She lighted the fire in the morning, cooked the food, and made the beds, while her sisters would be stringing flowers on a hank, or looking at themselves in the glass, or sitting with their hands across. "No one will ever come to marry us in this lonesome place," said the eldest one day; "so you and I," said she to the second sister, "may as well go seek our fortune." "That's the best word you ever spoke," said the other. "Bake our cake and kill our cock, mother, and away we go." Well, so she did; "And now, girls," said she, "which will you have, half this with my blessing, or the whole of it with my curse?" "Curse or no curse, mother, the whole of it is little enough."

Well they set off, and says Hairy Rouchy to her mother when they got to the end of the lane, "Mother, give me your blessing, and a quarter of the griddle cake, I must go after these girls, for I fear ill luck is in their road." She gave her her blessing and the whole of the cake, and she went off running, and soon overtook them. "Here's Hairy Rouchy," says the eldest, "she'll make a show of us. We'll tie her to this big stone." So they tied her to the big stone and went their way, but when they were a quarter of a mile further, there she was three perches behind them. Well, they were vexed enough, and the next clamp of turf they passed, they made her lie down, and piled every sod of it over her.

When they were a quarter of a mile further they looked back again, and there was the girl three perches behind them, and wern't they mad? To make a long story short, they fastened her in a pound, and they put the tying of the three smalls on her, and fastened her to a tree. The next quarter of a mile she was up by their side, and at last they were tired, and let her walk behind them.

Well, they walked and they walked till they were tired, and till the greyness of night came round them, and they saw a light at a distance. When they came up, what was it but a giant's house, and great sharp teeth were in the heads of himself, and his wife, and his three daughters. Well, they got lodging, and when sleep time was coming they were put into one bed, and the giant's daughters were put into another, and the foot of the daughters' bed touched the head of theirs. Well becomes my brave Hairy Rouchy, —when the giant's daughters were asleep, she took off the hair necklaces from her own neck and the necks of her sisters, and put them on the giant's daughters' necks, and she put their gold and silver and diamond necklaces on the necks of her sisters and herself, and then watched to see what would happen.

The giant and his wife were sitting by the fire, and says he, " Won't these girls make a fine meat pie for us to-morrow ?" " Won't they !" says she, and she smacked her lips, " but I'll have some trouble singeing that hairy one." " They are all asleep now," says he, and he called in his red-headed giolla. " Go and put them strangers out of pain," says he. " But how'll I know them from your daughters ?" says the giolla. " Very easy, they have only hair necklaces round their necks."

Well, you may all guess what happened. So the night faded away, and the morning came, and what did the giant see at the flight of darkness, when the gate was opened by the cow-boy, but Hairy Rouchy walking out through it after her two sisters. Down the stairs he came, five at a time, and out of the bawn he flew, and *mach go brath* (away for ever) with him after the girls. The eldest screamed out, and the second eldest screamed out, but the youngest took one under each arm, and if she did'nt lay leg to ground, you may call me a story-teller. She ran like the west wind, and the giant ran like the north wind; the sparks of fire he struck out of the stones hit her on the back, and the sparks of fire she struck out of the stones scorched his face. At last they came near the wide and deep river that divided his land from the land of the King of Spain, and into that land he daren't pass. Over the wide deep river went Hairy Rouchy with a high, very active bound, and after her went the giant. His heels touched the bank, and back into the water went his head and body. He dragged himself out on his own side, and sat down on the bank, and looked across, and this is what he said. "You're there Hairy Rouchy," says he. "No thanks to you for it," says she. "You got my three daughters killed," says he. "It was to save our own lives," says she. "When will you come to see me again?" says he. "When I have business," says she. "Divel be in your road," says he. "It's better pray than curse," says she.

The three girls went on till they came to the King of Spain's castle, where they were well entertained, and the King's eldest son and the eldest sister fell in love with one another, and the second son and the second sister fell in love with one another, and poor Hairy Rouchy fell in love with the youngest son, but he did'nt fall in love with her.

Well, the next day, when they were at breakfast, says the King to her, "Good was your deed at the giant's house, and if you only bring me the talking golden quilt that's covering himself and his wife, my eldest son may marry your eldest sister." "I'll try," says she; "worse than lose I can't."

So that night, when the giant and his wife were fast asleep, the quilt felt a hand pulling it off the bed. "Who are you?" says the quilt. "*Mishé*" (myself), says the girl,—and she pulled away. "Waken, master!" says the quilt; "some one is taking me away." "And who's taking you away?" says he. "It's Mishe that's doing it," says the quilt. "Then let Mishe stop his tricks, and not be disturbing us. "But I tell you, Mishe is carrying me off." "If Mishe says another word, I'll get up, and throw him in the fire." So the poor quilt had nothing to do but hold its tongue.

"But," says the giant's wife, after a few minutes, "maybe the divel bewitcht the quilt to walk off with itself." "Faith and maybe so," says the giant; "I'll get up and look." So he searched the room, and the stairs, and the hall, and the bawn, and the bawn gate was open. "*Milé mollachd*," says he; "Hairy Rouchy was here;" and to the road he took. But when he was on the hill she was in the hollow, and when he was in the hollow she was on the hill, and when he came to the hither side of the river she was on the thither. "You're there, Hairy Rouchy!" says he. "No thanks to you," says she. . . . . "You took away my speaking golden quilt," says he. "It was to get my eldest sister married," says she. "When will you come again?" . . . . "Divel be in your road," says he. "It's better pray than curse," says she; and the same night the speaking golden quilt was covering the King and Queen of Spain.

Well, the wedding was made, but there was little notice taken of poor Hairy Rouchy, and she spent a good part of the day talking to a poor travelling woman that she often relieved at home and that was come by *accidence* as far as Spain.

"So the next day, when they were at breakfast again, says the King, "Hairy Rouchy, if you bring me to-morrow morning the *chloive solais* (sword of light) that hangs at the giant's bed's head, my second son will marry your second sister." "I'll make the trial," says she; "worse than lose I can't."

Well, the next night the giant's wife was boiling his big pot of gruel, and Hairy Rouchy was sitting by the *chimbly* on the scraws that covered the ridge-pole, and dropping fistfuls of salt into the pot. "You put too much salt in this porridge," says the giant to his wife, when he was supping it. "I'm sure I did't put in more than four spoonfuls," says she. "Well, well, that was the right size; still it tastes mortial salty."

When he was in bed he cried out, "Wife, I'll be a piece of cured bacon before morning if I don't get a drink." "Oh, then, purshuin to the sup of water in the house," says she. "Well, call up the giolla out of the settle, and let him bring a pailful from the well." So the giolla got up in a bad humour, scratching his head, and went to the door with the pail in his hand. There was Hairy Rouchy by the jamb, and maybe she didn't dash fistfuls of sand and salt into his eyes. "Oh masther, masther," says he, the sky is as black as your hat, and it's pelting hailstones on me; I'll never find the well." "Here you onshuch, take the sword of light, and it will show you the way."

So he took the chloive solais, and made his way to the well, and while he was filling the pail he laid the sword on the ground. That was all the girl wanted. She snatched it up, waved it round her head, and the light flashed over hills and hollows. "If you're not into the house like a shot," says she, "I'll send your head half a mile away." The poor giolla was only too glad to get off, and she was soon flying like the wind to the river, and the giant hot foot after her. When she was in the hollow he was on the hill. . . . .

"You're a very good girl, indeed," says the King of Spain to Hairy Rouchy, the morning after the second marriage; "you deserve a reward. So bring me the giant's puckawn with the golden bells round his neck, as soon as you like, and you must get my youngest son for a husband. "But maybe he wont have me," says she. "Indeed an' I will," says the prince; "so good a sister can't make a bad wife." "But I'm all hairy and brown," says she. "That's no sin," says the prince.

Sure enough, the night after, she was hard and fast in the giant's out-house, stuffing the puckawn's bells with the marrow of the elder; and when she thought the job was well finished she was leading him out. She had a band on his mouth, but when my brave puck found he couldn't bawl, he took to rear and kick like a puck as he was. Out came the elder marrow from three of the bells, and the sound that came from them was enough to waken the dead. She drove him at his full speed before her, but after came the giant like a storm. She could escape him if she liked, but she would not return without puck, and bedad she was soon pinned and brought back to the giant's big kitchen. There was his wife and the giolla, and if he wasn't proud to show them his prisoner there's not a glove in Wexford.

"Now, ma'am," says he to her, "I have you safe after all the mischief you done me. If I was in your power what would you do to me?" "Oh wouldn't I tie you up to the ceiling in a sack, you ould tyrant, and go myself and giolla to the wood, cut big clubs, and break every bone in your body one after another. Then if there was any life left in you, we'd make a fire of the green boughs underneath, and stifle the little that was left out of you." "The very thing I'll do with you," says he.

So he put her in a sack, tied her up to the beam that went across the kitchen, and went off with the the giolla to the wood to cut down the clubs and green branches, leaving his wife to watch the prisoner. She expected to hear crying and sobbing from out of the sack, but the girl did nothing but shout and laugh. "Is it mad you are," says she, " and death so near you?" "Death indeed! Why, the bottom of the sack is full of diamonds, and pearls, and guineas, and there is the finest views all round me you ever see—castles, and lawns, and lakes, and the finest flowers." "Is it lies you're telling?" "Oh dickens a lie! If I'd let you up, but I won't, you'd see and feel it all."

But the giant's wife over-persuaded her, and when she was loosened, and got the other into the sack, she tied her hard and fast, ran to the out-house, threw a rope round the puckawn's neck, and he and she were soon racing like the wind towards the river. The giant and the giolla were soon back, and he wondered where his wife could be. But he saw the sack still full, and the two began to whack it like so many blacksmiths. "Oh Lord," says the poor woman, "it's myself that's here." "And to be sure it's yourself," says he; "here goes again." But she roared out, "Ah sure I'm your wife; don't kill me for goodness' sake!" "Be the laws," says the giolla, "it's the mistress. Oh, bad luck to you, Hairy Rouchy; this is your doing. Run and catch her, master, while I take the poor mistress down, and see what I can do for her." Off went the big fellow like a bow-arra, but when he came to this side of the river panting and puffing, there was the girl and his darling puckawn on the other side, and she ready to burst her sides with the laughing.

"You're there, my damsel." "No thanks, etc." So the scolding match went on to the end, and then says he, "If you were in my place, and I in yours now, what would you do?" "I'd stoop down and drink the river dry to get at you." But she didn't stop to see whether he was fool enough to take her advice, but led her goat to the palace. Oh, wasn't there great joy and clapping of hands when the golden bells were heard a ringing up the avenue, and into the big bawn? She didn't mind how any one looked but the youngest prince; and though he didn't appear very rejoiced, there was a kind smile on his face, and she was satisfied.

Well, the next morning, when they were all setting out to the church, and the bridegroom was mounted on his horse, and the bride getting into the coach, she asked him for leave to take the poor travelling woman in along with her. "It's a queer request," says he, "but do as you like; you must have some reason for it." Well, when all were dismounting or getting out of their coaches, he went to open the door for his bride, and the sight almost left his eyes; for there sitting *fornent* him was the most beautiful young woman he ever beheld. She had the same kind innocent look that belonged to Hairy Rouchy, but she had also the finest colour in her face, and neck, and hands, and her hair, instead of the tangled brake it used to be, was nicely *platted* and curled, and was the finest dark brown in the world.

Glad enough she was to see the joy and surprise in his face, and if they were not the happy bride and bridegroom I never saw one. When they were talking by themselves, she told him that an enchantment was laid on her when she was a child, and she was always to remain the fright she was, till some one would marry her for the sake of her disposition. The travelling woman was her guardian fairy in disguise. There were two unhappy marriages and one happy one in the King of Spain's family, and I'll let every one here guess which was which.

A LEGEND OF CLEVER WOMEN.

BEFORE Joan was married all her people had a high opinion of her. When Darby came to woo her, her mother told him in confidence that she could see the wind, and hear the flies when they coughed. Well, when they were at dinner the beer came short, and Joanna went down to the cellar to draw a gallon-full. She stayed awhile, and then her mother went to see what was keeping her. She wasn't coming back, and the father's and Darby's thirst was getting more troublesome; so the old man went after the rest. As he forgot to return, the bridegroom thought fit at last to try what had become of his new relations, and when he got inside the cellar, he found the whole of them sobbing and crying. "What in the world has happened, dear friends?" said he. "Oh nothing," says the mother, "but something terrible might happen only for the cleverness of my poor Joan. Do you see that loose stone in the vault just over the spigot? When my poor child was filling the gallon, that stone caught her eye, and she thought what a heartscald it would be when the little boy, that God will please to send to herself and yourself, would be filling a vessel, maybe when he'd be ten years old or so, and that stone tumble down and kill him dead. So how could she help clapping her hands an' roarin' an' bawlin' when the thought came into her head? and I'm sure her father an' meself would have the hard hearts not to feel for her." "Well, well," says Darby, "I'll soon put it out of the stone's power to do mischief." So he got on a stillion, and pulled it away, and they all dried their eyes and returned to their dinner.

Well, when they were living by themselves, Darby says one morning to his wife after breakfast, "You'll have my dinner ready at half-past twelve to the minute. You know I have to go to the town after it." "Never fear, Darby," says she; and sure enough she had a big black pudding hissing in the pan about ten minutes before she expected him. While she was watching it, the thought came into her mind that it would be a good thing to be drawing the beer while the pudding was frying. But while she was watching the beer falling into the jug, she heard them cry out, "The dog is running away with the pudding!" Out she flew like a racer, and after the dog with her; but when she had chased him two fields he was a whole field ahead of her, and she thought she might as well go back.

Poor Joan! when she came to the cellar door, the floor was covered three inches deep with the beer, the barrel was empty, but the jug was full any way. "We must make the best of a bad market," says she. "Darby would be vexed to see the cellar this way, and I must get out his drink whatever happens." So she emptied a sack of meal on the pool, and was delighted to see it was almost all sucked up. Then she laid the sack across to the barrel, and hardly wet her pumps, and would have had the full jug coming back only for a kick she happened to give it. Poor Darby had a poor dinner, but Joan was so heated, and so proud of her good management, that he hadn't the heart to scold her. She showed him how nicely all would have happened, and what a comfortable dinner she might have ready for him, only for the roguery of the dog when he found the door open, and how could she spare time to turn the cock when she heard the shout? Darby, however, began to suspect that she was not so clever as her father and mother said she was.

A week after he had to go to the town, and says he, just as he was setting out, "Joan, you must mind what I say to you. *Shan na Mo* (Jack of the Cows) will be apt to call while I'm away, for Browny, and Blacky, and Brackedy. He agreed to pay thirty pounds for them, but he's rather tricky; so don't let him get a hoof of one of them without paying the money on the nail." "I'll be careful," says Joan. Darby came back in the evening. "Well, Joan my darling, how did you succeed?" "Oh nicely. You'll never say after this that I wasn't clever. I think Shan is just as tricky as you said he was, but he didn't circumvent me." "Them cows," says he, "is dear enough, but I'll take 'em; what's a man but his word?" and he was driving them out at the bawn gate. "Oh stop!" says I, "you didn't give me the thirty pounds." "Didn't I," says he, "Well, what a memory I have! and, bedad," says he, rummaging his pockets, "I left the rowl of notes on the dresser coming out. Now I'll have the trouble of going for them. Ah! I wish my wife was as clever as you, Joan. I'd be a thousand pounds richer to-day. Happy is the man that owns you! Oh, this is what we can do, and save trouble. These three cows are mine. I'll leave you one in pledge till I send you the money this evening or to-morrow morning." "Well, see my cleverness! I kept the smallest because she'd eat the least till he'll send the money. Now what do you say to me, Darby?" "Indeed,

I'll say this to you. You are such a fool that I'll never lie a night by your side, till I find some other woman more foolish;" and he turned his back, and to the road with him.

The first foolish woman he found had no window to her mud-wall cabin, and the door was turned to the north. She was running with a sieve in her hands in and out, crying, "I have it now," and, "I haven't it now," till Darby asked her what she was doing. "And ain't I striving to carry the sunshine into the cabin, and I can never get it inside the door?" "Have you a pick-axe in the way?" "Yes, to be sure." "Well, I'll soon bring it in to you." He went to the wall next the sun, gave two or three strokes, and a grey streak was soon coming in, and a splash of light on the floor. "Oh, fortunate was the wind that drove you in my road! what will I be giving you for this good job?" "Ah, my good woman, all you're worth wouldn't be enough; I'll take nothing;" and he went on, saying to himself, "She is not more foolish than Joan."

He was going by a cabin, and such roaring and bawling as was coming out through the door! In he ran, and there was a man sitting on a chair, with a clean linen sack on his head and his shoulders, and his wife with a beetle, coming down on his head with the hammers of death, and he roaring like fifty bulls. "What are you doing, you wicked woman?" says Darby; "do you want to kill the poor man?" "Indeed, an' I don't, but I want to make a hole in this divel of a shirt to let his head and face up through it!" "Have you a scissors about you?" "To be sure; I'd be a purty housewife if I hadn't." Darby made a cut in the top of the bag, and the poor bruised head came out. "Oh, musha, wasn't it good fortune that drove you into the cabin! What'll we be giving you for your trouble?" "All you're worth wouldn't be enough; so I'll take nothing; *banacht lath!* I don't think she's worse than Joan. I'll go on."

The next adventure he met was in a widow-woman's bawn, where herself and a few neighbours were striving to lift up a big cow to the eaves of the cabin, and the poor animal kicking off their hats, and tearing their clothes with her hoofs. "God bless the men and their work!" says Darby. "God save you kindly," says they. "What are yous doing with the poor baste?" says he. "An' sure we're striving to get her up on the *tatch*," says the widow, "'till she makes a meal on all that fine grass that's growing on itself, and the scraws at the top." "Let her down," says he, "and may be we'll come on an easier plan. Give us a reaping-hook, if you have the like." So he got a ladder, and was soon down again with an armfull of the grass. "Well to be sure!" says the poor widow, "nothing bates the wit of man barring the bees. It was a good wind," &c., &c. "I don't think," says Darby, "she's a bit worse than Joan. My journey is not over."

Just as night fell, he went into a farm-house and put up for the night. The owner was a widow-woman that was after burying her third husband. The first two were such crooked disciples that she married a third to get the taste of them off her mouth, as she said. "Where do you come from, honest man?" says she to Darby, after supper. "I am from the *Gairdheen*" (Garden, the name of his farm.) "Oh, and are you from the GARDEN in earnest?" "Faith I am so; what do you admire about it?" "Oh, and may be you are acquainted with my poor husband, the last I mean, the others I'm sure never had the grace to get there." Darby now smelled a rat. "And what sort of a man was your last, and what was the name was on him?" "An' wasn't he poor Jack Miskella, the innocentest and little-good-for-est man that ever drew on a stocking? A child of three years old would buy and sell him any day he ever got up." "I know the man you mean, and have a message to you from him. He have no means of earning his bread, and his clothes is nearly worn out. So he does be begging at the good Christians' doors, and he bid me tell you, if you'd send him a comfortable suit of clothes, not forgetting a pair of double-soled brogues, you'd make a man of him; and if he had an ass or a small garran to carry him from one charitable house to another, he'd be as happy as a king, it 'ud be such an ease to his poor legs." "Ah, an' them's the very things he must have, my poor Jack! I suppose you'd like to be off early to him. The ass will be ready bridled and saddled in the stable, and the full suit will be laid out here on the kitchen table; and if you think they'd be of any use, there'll be a few guinea notes in the pockets." "Never mind the notes; every family does everything for itself in that country."

"I think," says Darby to himself next morning, "I've found a woman rather more foolish than poor Joan; so I'll go back to her." He did so, and they led such a life that whenever a loving couple are seen going together to Mass or market, every one says, "There goes Darby and Joan."

THE TWELVE WILD GEESE.

THERE was once a King and Queen that lived very happily together, and they had twelve sons and not a single daughter. We are always wishing for what we haven't, and don't care for what we have, and so it was with the Queen. One day in winter, when the bawn was covered with snow, she was looking out of the parlour window, and saw there a calf that was just killed by the butcher, and a raven standing near it. "Oh," says she, "if I had only a daughter with her skin as white as that snow, her cheeks as red as that blood, and her hair as black as that raven, I'd give away every one of my twelve sons for her." The moment she said the word, she got a great fright, and a shiver went through her, and in an instant after, a severe-looking old woman stood before her. "That was a wicked wish you made," said she, "and to punish you it will be granted. You will have such a daughter as you desire, but the very day of her birth you will lose your other children." She vanished the moment she said the words.

And that very way it turned out. When she expected her delivery, she had her children all in a large room of the palace, with guards all round it, but the very hour her daughter came into the world, the guards inside and outside heard a great whirling and whistling, and the twelve princes were seen flying one after another out through the open window, and away like so many arrows over the woods. Well, the king was in great grief for the loss of his sons, and be would be very enraged with his wife if he only knew that she was so much to blame for it.

Everyone called the little princess Snow-white-and-Rose-red on account of her beautiful complexion. She was the most loving and loveable child that could be seen anywhere. When she was twelve years old she began to be very sad and lonely, and to torment her mother, asking her about her brothers that she thought were dead, for none up to that time ever told her the exact thing that happened them. The secret was weighing very heavy on the Queen's conscience, and as the little girl persevered in her questions, at last she told her. "Well, mother," said she, "it was on my account my poor brothers were changed into wild geese, and are now suffering all sorts of hardship; before the world is a day older, I'll be off to seek them, and try to restore them to their own shapes."

The King and Queen had her well watched, but all was no use. Next night she was getting through the woods that surrounded the palace, and she went on and on that night, and till the evening of next day. She had a few cakes with her, and she got nuts, and *mugoreens* (fruit of the sweet briar) and some sweet crabs as she went along. At last she came to a nice wooden house just at sunset. There was a fine garden round it, full of the handsomest flowers, and a gate in the hedge. She went in, and saw a table laid out with twelve plates, and twelve knives and forks, and twelve spoons, and there were cakes, and cold wild fowl, and fruit along with the plates, and there was a good fire, and in another long room there were twelve beds. Well, while she was looking about her she heard the gate opening, and footsteps along the walk, and in came twelve young men, and there was great grief and surprise on all their faces when they laid eyes on her. "Oh, what misfortune sent you here?" said the eldest. "For the sake of a girl we were obliged to leave our father's court, and be in the shape of wild geese all day. That's twelve years ago, and we took a solemn oath that we would kill the first young girl that came into our hands. It's a pity to put such an innocent and handsome girl as you are out of the world, but we must keep our oath." "But," said she, "I'm your only sister that never knew anything about this till yesterday; and I stole away from our father's and mother's palace last night to find you out and relieve you if I can." Every one of them clasped his hands, and looked down on the floor, and you could hear a pin fall till the eldest cried out, "A curse light on our oath! what shall we do?" "I'll tell you that," said an old woman that appeared at the instant among them. "Break your wicked oath which no one should keep. If you attempted to lay an uncivil finger on her I'd change you into twelve *booliaun buis* (stalks of ragweed), but I wish well to you as well as to her. She is appointed to be your deliverer in this way. She must spin and knit twelve shirts for you out of bog down, to be gathered by her own hands on the moor just outside of the wood. It will take her five years to do it, and if she once speaks, or laughs, or cries the whole time, you will have to remain wild geese by day till you're called out of the world. So take care of your sister; it is worth your while." The fairy then vanished, and it was only a strife with the brothers to see who would be first to kiss and hug their sister.

So for three long years the poor young princess was occupied pulling bog down, spinning it, and knitting it into shirts, and at the end of the three years she had eight made. During all that time, she never spoke a word, nor laughed, nor cried; the last was the hardest to refrain from. One fine day she was sitting in the garden spinning, when in sprung a fine greyhound and bounded up to her, and laid his paws on her shoulder, and licked her forehead and her hair. The next minute a beautiful young prince rode up to the little garden gate, took off his hat, and asked for leave to come in. She gave him a little nod, and in he walked. He made ever so many apologies for intruding, and asked her ever so many questions, but not a word could he get out of her. He loved her so much from the first moment, that he could not leave her till he told her he was king of a country just bordering on the forest, and he begged her to come home with him, and be his wife. She couldn't help loving him as much as he did her, and though she shook her head very often and was very sorry to leave her brothers, at last she nodded her head, and put her hand in his, she knew well enough that the good fairy and her brothers would be able to find her out. Before she went she brought out a basket holding all her bog-down, and another holding the eight shirts. The attendants took charge of these, and the prince placed her before him on his horse. The only thing that disturbed him while riding along was the displeasure his stepmother would feel at what he had done. However he was full master at home, and as soon as he arrived he sent for the bishop, got his bride nicely dressed, and the marriage was celebrated, the bride answering by signs. He knew by her manners she was of high birth, and no two could be fonder of each other.

The wicked stepmother did all she could to make mischief, saying she was sure she was only a woodman's daughter; but nothing could disturb the young king's opinion of his wife. In good time the young queen was delivered of a beautiful boy, and the king was so glad he hardly knew what to do for joy. All the grandeur of the christening and the happiness of the parents tormented the bad woman more than I can tell you, and she determined to put a stop to all their comfort. She got a sleeping posset given to the young mother, and while she was thinking and thinking how she could best make away with the child, she saw a wicked-looking wolf in the garden, looking up at her, and licking his chops. She lost no time, but snatched the child from the arms of the sleeping woman, and pitched it out. The beast caught it in his mouth, and was over the garden fence in a minute. The wicked woman then pricked her own fingers, and dabbled the blood round the mouth of the sleeping mother.

Well, the young king was just then coming into the big bawn from hunting, and as soon as he entered the house, she beckoned to him, shed a few crocodile tears, began to cry and wring her hands, and hurried him along the passage to the bedchamber.

Oh, wasn't the poor king frightened when he **saw** the queen's mouth **bloody**, and missed his child? It would take two hours to tell you the devilment of the old queen, the confusion, and fright, and grief of young king and queen, the bad opinion he began to feel of his wife, and the struggle she had to keep down her bitter sorrow, and not give way to it by speaking or lamenting. The young king would not allow any one to be called, and ordered his step-mother to give out that the child fell from the mother's arms at the window, and that a wild beast ran off with it. The wicked woman pretended to do so, but she told underhand to everybody she spoke to, what the king and herself saw in the bedchamber.

The young queen was the most unhappy woman in the three kingdoms for a long time, between sorrow for her child, and her husband's bad opinion; still she neither spoke nor cried, and she gathered bog-down and went on with the shirts. Often the twelve wild geese would be seen lighting on the trees in the park or on the smooth sod, and looking in at her windows. So she worked on to get the shirts finished, but another year was at an end, and she had the twelfth shirt finished except one arm, when she was obliged to take to her bed, and a beautiful girl was born.

Now the king was on his guard, and he would not let the mother and child be left alone for a minute; but the wicked woman bribed some of the attendants, set others asleep, gave the sleepy posset to the queen, and had a person watching to snatch the child away, and kill it. But what should she see but the same wolf in the garden looking up, and licking his chops again? Out went the child, and away with it flew the wolf, and she smeared the sleeping mother's mouth and face with blood, and then roared, and bawled, and cried out to the king and to everybody she met, and the room was filled, and every one was sure the young queen had just devoured her own babe.

The poor mother thought now her life would leave her. She was in such a state she could neither think nor pray, but she sat like a stone, and worked away at the arm of the twelfth shirt.

The king was for taking her to the house in the wood where he found her, but the stepmother, and the lords of the court, and the judges would not hear of it, and she was condemned to be burned in the big bawn at three o'clock the same day. When the hour drew near, the king went to the farthest part of his palace, and there was no more unhappy man in his kingdom at that hour.

When the executioners came and led her off, she took the pile of shirts in her arms. There were still a few stitches wanted, and while they were tying her to the stake, she still worked on. At the last stitch she seemed overcome and dropped a tear on her work, but the moment after she sprang up, and shouted out, "I am innocent; call my husband!" The executioners stayed their hands, except one wicked-disposed creature who set fire to the faggot next him, and while all were struck in amaze, there was a rushing of wings, and in a moment the twelve wild geese were standing round the pile. Before you could count twelve, she flung a shirt over every bird, and there in the twinkling of an eye were twelve of the finest young men that could be collected out of a thousand. While some were untying their sister, the eldest, taking a strong stake in his hand, struck the busy executioner such a blow that he never needed another.

While they were comforting the young queen, and the king was hurrying to the spot, a fine-looking woman appeared among them holding the babe on one arm and the little prince by the hand. There was nothing but crying for joy, and laughing for joy, and hugging and kissing, and when any one had time to thank the good fairy, who in the shape of a wolf, carried the child away, she was not to be found. Never was such happiness enjoyed in any palace that ever was built, and if the wicked queen and her helpers were not torn by wild horses they richly deserved it.

THE WONDERFUL CAKE.

A MOUSE, a rat, and a little red hen once lived together in the same cabin, and one day the little red hen said, "Let us bake a cake and have a feast." "Let us," says the mouse; and "let us," says the rat. "Who'll go get the wheat ground?" says the hen. "I wont," says the mouse; "I won't," says the rat; "I'll go myself," says the little red hen. "Who'll make the cake?" "I won't," says the mouse; "I won't," says the rat; "I will myself," says the little red hen. . . . . "Who'll eat the cake?" "I will," says the mouse; "I will," says the rat; "Dickens a bit you shall," says the little red hen. Well, while the hen was putting over her hand to it, *magh go brath* with it out of the door, and after it with the three housekeepers.

When it was running away, it went by a barn full of thrashers, and they asked it where it was running. "Oh," says it, "I'm running away from the mouse, the rat, and the little red hen, and from you too if I can." So they piked away after it with their flails, and it run and it run till it came to a ditch full of ditchers, and they asked it where it was running. . . . . . "Oh, I'm running away from the mouse, the rat, and the little red hen, and from a barn full of thrashers, and from you too if I can." Well they all ran after it along with the rest till it came to a well full of washers, and they asked the same question, and it returned the same answer, and after it they went. At last it came to a ford where it met with a fox, who asked where it was running. "Oh, I'm running away from the mouse, the rat, and the little red hen, from a barn full of thrashers, a ditch full of ditchers, a well full of washers, a crumply-horned cow, a saddled-backed sow, and from you too if I can." "But you can't cross the ford," says the fox. "And can't you carry me over?" says the cake. "What'll you give me?" says the fox. "A kiss at Christmas, and an egg at Easter," says the cake. "Very well," says the fox—"up with you."

So he sat on his *currabingo* with his nose in the air, and the cake got up by his tail till it sat on his crupper. "Now over with you," says the cake. "You're not high enough." Then it scrambled up on his shoulder. "Up higher still," says he, "you wouldn't be safe there." "Am I right now?" says the cake, when it was on his head. "Not quite," says he; "you'll be safer on the ridge pole of my nose." "Well," says the cake, "I think I can go no further." "Oh, yes," says he, and he shot it up in the air, caught it in his mouth, and sent it down the red lane.

THE FALSE BRIDE.

THERE was once a king and a queen that loved each other very much, and they had a beautiful and kindly dispositioned daughter. But the queen was taken ill, and when she was dying she called her daughter alone to her bedside, and fastened a woven ring of hair, and silk, and gold thread on her left arm, just under her shoulder, and said, "Now, my dear daughter, you must be very careful not to let any womankind get possession of that ring. It was given to me by a good fairy when you were an infant, and she said that as long as you wore it, no one could do you any real harm. But if once it was taken from you, she that took it would command you in every way, and if she was as ugly as sin, you should take her appearance, and it was in her power to take yours, the moment the change was made."

When the queen was dead, one lady of the court, who had rather an ugly looking daughter, became very loving to the young princess, and she spoke of the king's loss so feelingly, and pitied him so much, that the princess thought it would be the finest thing in the world if her father would make her his second wife. So she was evermore speaking of the lady's goodness of heart, and nice manners, and she plagued her father so, that to get rid of the bother he married the cunning lady at last. The first dinner they all took together, the new queen gave wine to the princess, and water to her own girl; the next, she gave them both wine, and the third, the poor princess had to put up with water. By degrees she turned her father very much against her, telling him all manner of lies and stories, and when there were great parties she would not be allowed to join in them, because the young nobles and princes would dance oftener with her, and entertain her with discourse much oftener than her step-sister, for this one had a bad temper as well as an ugly face.

So the poor young lady spent a great deal of her time in her chamber, or when the weather was fine, out in the park, sometimes walking, and sometimes sitting under the trees and doing needle-work. One day she was hemming a handkerchief, with her little dog on one side and her work basket on the other, and a voice that she thought belonged to one of the gentlemen of the court said, "Who are you hemming the handkerchief for, fair lady?" "For the King of Norway's son," said she by way of joke. "Then I am a happy man," said the voice, "for I am that person." She looked up, and all the blood in her veins rushed into her face, for she saw she was speaking with a noble-looking, and well-formed, and handsome young man with rich clothes on him. I won't tire you with all the confusion at first, and the charming discourse that followed; but, to make a long story short, she ran home, and the prince soon followed her, and paid his respects to her father, and asked for her in marriage. Well, he didn't get a refusal, but the step-mother and step-sister were as mad as you please at the preference that was shown her.

The young prince soon returned home to prepare for the wedding, and in a week's time the princess was sent after him, and a company of gentlemen and attendants went with her, to do her honour and protect her from accidents, and her step-sister went also, out of respect as she said. But she got some lessons in private from her mother.

One day they stopped at a nobleman's house, and as it was hot weather the princess, and the step-sister, and the step-sister's maid went down to a summer-house that was on the edge of the lake to bathe. When the three were in the water, the step-sister took hold of the princess by the arm, and said with a wicked tone, and her teeth almost closed, "Loose that platted ring from your arm, and give it to me quietly, or we will drown you here without pity." She begged and prayed for mercy, but all to no use. She forgot that they could do her no harm while she had the ring, and so, to save her young life, she unclasped it, and fastened it on the other's arm. The moment it was on the appearances of both were changed, and the princess got the ugly look of her step-sister, who was now as beautiful as she had been a minute before. "Now," says the wicked girl, "swear that you will never tell to any human being, young or old, what has happened, or drowned you shall be." So, to save her life, she took the oath.

They went on again after their rest; the step-sister as beautiful as the lily and rose, and the princess as ordinary in feature as if she were a tinker's daughter, but their dispositions remained the same as before. No one saw the difference but the little dog, and now he would not come near the false princess, whatever patting or coaxing she could try. The young prince of Norway was right glad to welcome his bride to her new home, but after a little he was surprised at the tone of her voice, and the coarse kind of talk she used, and her bad temper.

The wedding was celebrated, and I'll leave you to feel for the poor princess that day and night and for a week after. The bride got little comfort in her new life. She had great grandeur, but she saw that her husband didn't care for her; he found such a difference in her discourse from what he heard from her at her father's palace, and there was nothing good-natured, or witty, or pleasant in all that came out of her lips. Every one liked the poor ugly sister, she was so cheerful and kind with gentle and simple. Even the prince would chat as long with her as his wife would let him, and the old king grew as fond of her as if she was his daughter.

This did not at all please the bride, and so she told the princess to make ready for her return. She was to set out in three days, and every one in the court was sorry, but so it should be. Well, the next day, a young boy that was employed in the kitchen watched the old king when he was taking a walk in the grove, and says he, "I ask pardon, but I could not help telling your majesty what I heard the young queen's sister saying to her little dog last night when she thought every one was asleep. She went out in the garden, and I thought it so queer that I crept after in the shade, till she went into the summer-house, and sobbed and cried as if her heart was going to break. 'My poor faithful little dog,' said she, ' little does my father or the young prince that should be my husband, know what my wicked step-sister did to me; how she and her maid went about drowning me till I was forced to take the platted ring off my own arm and put it on hers, and how our appearances were changed from that moment; and that she who lies by his side now is not his own love at all, but the wicked daughter of a wicked mother. I am obliged by a solemn oath not to tell this treachery to any human being, but if I did not speak about it my heart would break, and so I tell it to you, my dear little dog.' And then she lamented her fate so bitterly that I couldn't help crying. For fear she should find out that she was heard, I did not stir till I saw her going up the walk and into the castle."

"Don't say a word of this to any one at your peril," said the old king to the boy, "and you shall be well rewarded for your discovery." He went in and requested the bride and bridegroom and the princess to come into his own private room, and there, while all were wondering what he had to say, he asked the bride if she wore on her left arm under the shoulder a platted ring of hair, and silk, and gold-thread. She reddened up, but did not deny it, as the bridegroom saw it more than once. "Will you please to let all the present company look at it?" said he. Well, she was very unwilling, but thought better to comply. "Oblige me now, ma'am," said he, "by opening the clasp." "I don't know how," said she. "That's true, at any rate," said the king. "Perhaps, madam," said he to the princess, "you know the plan." "Oh, you forsworn creature!" said the bride, "aren't you afraid of breaking your solemn oath?" "She broke no oath," said the king. "She told her dismal story to her little dog in the summer-house last night, and he that overheard it told it to me. Dear daughter," said he to her, "open the clasp." "She shall not," cried the wicked bride, "while I have life or strength;" and she stamped like a fury. Three of the guards were called in, and very hard they found it to keep her quiet while the princess loosened the clasp. There she was the next moment as ugly as sin, and her own beautiful colour and features came back to the true princess. I need not tell you how the wicked girl was sent back to her mother, bound hand and foot, and how the king banished them both from his kingdom, and threatened to have them torn by wild horses if ever they dared to return. Well, another marriage was soon celebrated, and if there wasn't joy and happiness at it, there's no such thing in the world. And if yourselves and myself were living within ten miles of the palace, I'm sure we'd get an invitation.

THE END OF THE WORLD.

A HEN was standing under a hazel-tree one day, and a nut fell on her tail. Away she ran to the Cock, and says she, "Cocky Locky, the end of the world is come." "How do you know, Henny Penny?" says he. "Oh, a nut fell on my tail just now." "If that be so, we have nothing for it but to run away." So they ran till they met the Duck. "Oh, Ducky Lucky, the end of the world is come." "How do you know, Cocky Locky?" "Oh, a nut fell just now on Henny Penny's tail." "If that be so, we must run for it." When they were pegging off, they met the Goose. "Oh, Goosey Poosey, the end of the world is come." "How do you know, Ducky Lucky?" "A nut fell on Henny Penny's tail just now." "If that be the case, we are done for." They met the Fox. "Oh, Foxy Coxy, the world is come to an end." "How do you know that, Goosey Poosey?" "Oh, a nut fell on Henny Penny's tail." "Then let us be off." So they got into the wood, and says Foxy Coxy, "Let me count if all are safe. I, Foxy Coxy, one; you, Goosey Poosey, two; Ducky Lucky, three; Cocky Locky, four; Henny Penny, five. Number five, I'll put you in a safe place where the end of the world won't hurt you." So he took Henny Penny behind a bush and put her out of pain. "Now," says he, coming back, "let us count if all the rest are safe. I, Foxy Coxy, one; you, Goosey Poosey, two; &c. &c. Number four, I'll put you in a place where you'll be safe when the end of the world comes." He took him behind another bush, &c. &c. &c. "Now let me see if all the rest are here. I, Foxy Coxy, one; &c. &c. &c;" and so on till he put the fear of the world's end out of every one of them.

THE THREE GIFTS.

THERE was once a widow woman and she had only one son, an innocent slob of a boy, and one summer when the food was scarce and dear, Jack said he'd not be a burthen to his mother any longer, but go and look for service. Well, the poor mother gave him her best blessing, and he began to make the road short. He walked all day till the heel of the evening, and then he took up at a farmer's house where he got his supper and a bed. All the talk of the family, the whole evening, was about outwitting people in making bargains, and how every one chuckled while he was telling how he passed off an old useless horse for a young one, or got a good price for a regular fowler of a pig. And the women were as bad as the men, boasting of how they cheated customers by passing off layers of bad butter under the good, and selling musty eggs for fresh, and I don't know all. The very old couple laughed at the children telling how they won pins and buttons by cheatery at pitch and toss and such games. Jack wondered at the sort of people he got among, but he was in no danger of falling in love with their ways.

Well, as roguish as they appeared, they were not without good nature. They gave him a good supper of potatoes, milk, and butter, and the only harm I wish King George is, that he may never have worse. They gave him a quarter of a barley griddle-cake next day, and he continued his quest. Late in the evening he came out on a common that had in the middle of it a rock or a great pile of stones overgrown with furze bushes, and, when he came up, there was a dwelling-house, and a cow-house, and a goat's-house, and a pig-stye all scooped out of the rock, and the cows were going into the byre, and the goats into their house, but the pigs were grunting and bawling before the door.

There was a comely old woman leaning over the half-door, scolding the pigs for being so impatient. Jack bade her the time of the evening, and she gave him back his good manners, and said if he wished to rest for the night he was welcome. There was nothing Jack liked better. So he got a good supper, and an offer to give him good wages if he stopped to mind her live stock, and the little plot of potatoes and corn that was sown.

So he agreed to try a quarter, and never was a quarter spent pleasanter. He looked after the puckawn and his twelve goats, the ram and sheep, and the black cattle, reaped the little plot of corn, and weeded the potato drills. His mistress and himself had never a cross word. She wasn't a fidget, and Jack was not lazy, and he'd often catch himself saying, "Our cows and our goats," as if he was partly a master, and she never thought the worse of him for it. At last the quarter came to an end, and his mistress bade him go home and see his mother, and come back to her if he liked. "Here's the wages I'll give you," said she, laying a hen on the table. "Do not ask it to do anything till you reach home; then throw some oats on the table, and say, 'Hen, hen, lay your eggs.'"

Jack knew the woman's good heart, and took away the hen as contented as if he got ten pounds. He got lodging at the same house as before, and they asked him ever so many questions, chiefly about the wages. He was such a slob of a fellow that the smallest child in the house was able to turn him inside out, so he acknowledged that the only wages he got for the quarter was the hen. "Oh, but you're the divel's own *gommula* of a Jack," says the man of the house, "for taking such wages. Put the carkeen on the table, and let us see what she can do." "Give us a handful of oats," says Jack. The oats was spilled out, and Jack said the words he was told, and the hen began to pick and to lay golden eggs as fast as you could reckon them, and such looks as every one gave, and such opening of eyes and clucking of tongues, and ohs! and ahs! no one ever heard in one place. When she laid about a score of eggs, Jack thought it was enough for one time, and he took all and bade the *banatigh* hold out her apron.

Every one paid Jack a great deal of respect the rest of the night. He asked leave to go to the barn when he felt himself sleepy, but dickens a foot they'd let him. He was put to sleep in a feather bed in one of the rooms below the parlour, and the hen was provided with a nice nest alongside of him. After a good breakfast next day they filled his pocket with a split cake and plenty of butter inside of it. When the hugging and kissing between himself and his mother was over, says she, "Jack, asthore, did you bring anything home with you?" "Faith, an' I did, mother," says he. "There's a hen that will make our fortune." "Hen *inagh!* *musha* what great value is the finest hen in Ireland!" "You'll see, mother, after you give her some oats on the table." The oats were spilled, and Jack said the same words as before, "Hen, hen, lay your eggs," but she went on picking, and not an *iotum* of an egg did she lay. "Well, Jack, my poor fellow, you were a *gaum* before you went to travel and you are a *gaum* after it. "Mother," says Jack, "I was deceived, that's all; but I'll try my fortune again." He took up at the farmer's house, and told how the hen wouldn't lay a single golden egg for him at his mother's. "What hen?" said they. "The one that laid the twenty golden eggs on that table." "Oh, my poor fellow, it's a dream you had the same night. The hen you had with you never laid an egg of any kind while she was here," and Jack didn't know what to think. He returned to his old mistress, and told her what happened him. "Couldn't you take my advice, Jack, and not try what your hen would do till you got home? The hen now at your mother's is not the one you took from here." "Lord!" says he, "would the dacent people that lodged and fed me do such a mean act?" and he began to think. "No help for misfortunes, Jack," says his mistress. "Go to your work, and we'll see what luck's in store for you in another quarter's time."

So he worked away like a May boy, and the cows, and goats, and sheep seemed all glad to see him again, for he was always a good head to them. But the old lady didn't keep him more than a week till she popped him home. "Here, Jack," says she, "is a table-cloth, but you are not to open it till you get home to your mother. Then spread it on the table, and say 'Table-cloth, do your duty,' and if you don't be surprised, I'm not speaking to you." Jack set out, and got lodging again at the same house, but he took good care not to show his treasure; he kept it folded round his body. Well, they began to joke on him about his dream, and to ask him what new prize he got. He held out a long time, but one of the children peeped under his coat, and saw the cloth. Well, they gave him no ease, but undervalued the article, and ridiculed him till at last out of bravery he spread it on the table, and cried out, "Table-cloth, do your duty." In a moment it was covered with dishes, and plates, and jugs, and tumblers, and knives and forks, all of pure gold, and the nicest meat and loaves were on the dishes, and sweet wine and ale in the jugs and tumblers. Every one was amazed, and Jack was not slow in asking them to fall to. They didn't need much pressing, and when all were satisfied, Jack insisted that the mistress of the house should put up all the gold vessels in her cupboard.

He was put to sleep in the same feather bed, and his cloth was put under his pillow by the mistress, and he got his bread and butter for the road, and his mother laughed at him when the table-cloth would do no more for him than the hen; and the farmer's family laughed worse when he came back; they called it his second dream; and so he returned very low-spirited to his old mistress that lived under the bushy rocks.

"Jack," says she, "I see nothing can be done for you nor for any one that can't say no, nor stand a jest. All my gifts are spent but one, and that's no great thing. Such as it is you may take it. Whenever you say 'Stick, do your duty,' you will very likely see something you didn't expect. You are always welcome to come back to me; but I'll give you no more wonderful presents. I'll give you just five pounds a quarter, as long as you stay with me; but first go back this one time more."

Jack got lodging in the same house, but he took no care to hide his stick, and I don't think any of them set any value on it more than himself. So they spoke of one thing and another, but though they pretended to feel no curiosity about what the stick could do, the discourse always came back to it. "Well," says Jack at last, "as I showed you the virtue of the other gifts, or dreamed I showed them (maybe I'm only dreaming now), I wont be a churl about this. Stick, do your duty." Oh, the moment he said the words, the stick flew from the head and shoulders of one to the head and shoulders of another, whacking, and cracking, and banging, and everyone roaring out, "Murdher, murdher!" and such a piece of confusion was never seen before under one roof. No one could get more than a rub or two at his bruises when his turn came round again. And it was one chorus of roaring and bawling. "Oh, Jack honey," says the woman of the house, "stop this mischief of a stick, and you must have your hen again." "But you know, ma'am, it was only a dream." "Dream or no dream, here she is." "Stick, stick, will that do?" said Jack, but it only went on throuncing harder than ever. "Well, Jack, here is the cloth also, and now stop it for goodness' sake." Stop it did like shot, at Jack's bidding, and came back to Jack's hand, but it was long before the groans and moans were at an end.

Jack would not sleep under the roof of such people. He rested in the barn the rest of the night on a good pile of straw, and next evening he was at home. You can hardly imagine the mother's surprise when she saw the hen lay golden eggs, and the cloth covered with gold vessels. Every one that was in need was the better of Jack's good luck; but in the beginning he did as much harm as service with his generosity to lazy and wicked creatures, but he learned wisdom all in good time. He and his mother drove in a carriage to the common where the good fairy lived; the common was there, and so was the rock with all the bushes, but neither house, nor mistress, nor the sheep, nor the cows, nor the *puckawn*, nor his troop of goats.

THE UNLUCKY MESSENGER.

THERE was once a farmer's wife that had a servant boy, and this poor boy's memory wasn't very good, nor indeed was himself bright in any way. She sent him one day to the butcher's in the next town for some hearts and livers and lights, and gave him a shilling. "But," said she, "I'm afraid you won't remember what I'm sending for." "Oh faith I will, ma'am," says he, "I'll be saying 'em the whole way, hearts and livers and lights;—hearts and livers and lights." "Well, do so, Jack, and maybe you'll succeed this time."

Jack went on repeating his message like a May-boy, till

he met a man that was returning home from a sea-voyage. His face was as yellow as a kite's claw, and just as he was passing Jack he gave him a slap in the jaw that almost knocked him down. "What's that for?" says poor Jack. "What was I doing to you?" "You mischievous brat, I can hardly keep my heart liver and lights from flying out of my mouth I'm so sea-sick, and the very mention of them is almost after turning me inside out." "Well, and what am I to be saying?" "Why, if you can't keep your tongue easy, say 'May they never come up!'" "Very well," says Jack. "Hearts—no, may they never come up, may they never come up!"

He was passing by a field where men were planting potatoes, and the first of them that heard him, jumped over the ditch and began to kick poor Jack. "Oh! what's that for? Sure I'm doin' no harm to yez." "Do you call that bad prayer, no harm, you thief? instead of saying, like a good neighbour, 'Two hundred this year; three hundred next year.'" "Oh, very well," says Jack, "I'll say that to please you," and he went on saying, "Two hundred this year; three hundred next year."

Well, a funeral was entering the churchyard just as Jack went by repeating his last lesson. "Oh, you nasty Turk!" says an old woman, "is them the prayers you're saying for the poor corpse's sowl, wishing for so many deaths?" "I'm not wishing for any one's death, God forbid!" "Then don't be repatin' them hathenish words." "And what words will I be repatin' if you please, ma'am?" "Any good prayer at all, suppose, 'Peace be with him!'" "Anything to please you, ma'am.—Peace be with him; peace be with him!"

He was passing by a farmer's bawn just as a fox was skelpin' away with a chicken in his mouth, and the whole family after him. While they kept on shouting, he kept on saying, "Peace be with him; peace be with him!"—"Oh, the d——pace you!" says the man of the house; "what a nice thing to wish for the red thief!" "An' what ought I say?" "If you must say anything, let it be "Hang the brute!"" "Oh, very well, one thing's as good as another. Hang the brute; hang the brute!"

A poor woman was getting along, and striving to keep her drunken husband from falling. When she heard what Jack was saying, she laid the man down easy by the side of the road, flew on Jack, knocked off his hat, boxed his ears for him, and pulled his hair. "Musha, ma'am, what's that for?" says Jack. "It's for what you said to my poor husband," says the woman, "an' he the best man in the five townlands, only when he's overtaken." "An' I wish you hadn't overtaken me; and what ought I to say, to please you?" "Oh, any good wish at all. 'May you never be separated,' will do." "Well, well! May you never be separated; may you never be separated."

The road was going by the edge of a bog, when what should he see but two men down in a deep hole, and one striving to drag the other out. When the strongest heard what he was saying, he cried out, "Stop there till I go up to you." And as sure as he did get up, he gave poor Jack a good beating. "Musha, musha!" says the poor fellow, "I'm doing what everybody is bidding me, and everybody is throuncin' me, and what's it all for?" "It's for your bad wishes, it is." "And what do you wish me to pray for?" "Say, 'One out; may the other soon be out.'" "Oh, very well."

He was saying as hard as he could, "One out; may the other be soon out!" when he met a man blind of one eye. Well, he was so mad he fell on Jack, and all he got before was only a flay-bite to what he suffered from this customer. "Ah, what are you baten' me this way for?" says the poor fellow. "For your impedence, and your bad prayers," says he. "And what am I to be saying then?" says Jack. "I'd advise you to be saying nothing at all." "Very well: nothing at all; nothing at all," went on Jack repeating till he came to the butcher's. "Well, my man, what do you want?" "Nothing at all; nothing at all." "Well, take it, and be off with yourself." "Oh, but I want something for the mistress." "What is it?" "Dickens a bit of me knows. I said so many *raimshogues* along the road, it's got out of my head. Nothing at all! One out; may the other soon be out! Hang the brute! Two hundred this year, &c., &c. Oh! *begonies*, I'll never be able to recollect it." "What did your mistress give you?" "A shillin'." "Give me the shillin', and I'll give you what you want." He did so. "Open your fist." He opened it, and the butcher put his mouth down into it, and I needn't say what he left behind him. He shut the fingers down on it again. "Now don't open your fist for your life till you get home to your mistress. She'll find what she wants inside of your fingers and thumb. Don't let a hare catch you till you're inside the house." Jack did as he was bid, and it's meself that's glad I wasn't standing in his shoes that day, when the mistress was lambasting him.

THE MAID IN THE COUNTRY UNDER GROUND.

THERE was once a man that was left a widower with a good and handsome daughter; but he thought fit to marry a widow, a very bad woman, who had a daughter as wicked as herself. They did all they could, by telling lies on her, to persuade her father to turn her away, but he would not. So one day that she was sent to the draw-well her step-mother came behind her, and threw her head foremost into it. She gave herself up for dead; but wasn't she surprised, after her breath was stopped for a while, to find herself lying in a green meadow, with a bright sun and blue sky over her? Well, she walked on till she came to a hedge, that was so old it was not able to bear up a bird. "I'm old and worn, fair maid," said the hedge; "step lightly over me." "That I will do with pleasure, poor hedge," said she. So she stepped so gently and lightly over, that not a twig was stirred. "I'll do you a good turn another time," said the hedge.

She went on a while till she came to where an oven stood with a hot fire under it, and all at once the loaves spoke. "Take us out, take us out, fair maiden. We're baking for seven years, and now we'll be all burned if you don't release us." So she took the shovel, opened the door, and laid them nicely side by side on the grass. "Now take one of us with you," said the loaves, "and good luck be in your road." She went on, and found a poor woman sitting on a stone, and crying with the hunger. She gave her the greater part of her loaf, and went on till she met a flight of sparrows sitting on a block, and they all chattered out, "Some crumbs, fair maid; some crumbs, fair maid, or we'll all be dead with the hunger. It's seven years since we got a good meal." So she crumbled the rest of the bread, and they all cried, "Some day, fair maid, this good will be surely repaid."

She next passed by an apple tree, and the branches were bent down to the ground with the fruit. "Shake me, shake me, fair maid; it's seven years since I was shaken before." So she gently shook the tree and the boughs, and gathered all into a nice heap round the trunk. "Take some in your hand and eat them," said the tree; I'll remember this deed some day." The next she met was a ram, with his wool all trailing on the ground behind him. "Shear me, fair maid," said he, "for I wasn't shorn for seven long years." So she laid his head on her knee, and clipped him so nice, that he cried out when she was walking away, "Fair maid, I'll do you a good turn for this some day." The next she met was a cow, with her poor *elder* (udder) so full that it was trailing on the ground. "Milk me, fair maid," said she; "I wasn't milked these seven long years." So she did, and the cow licked her, and *mooed* after her, "Fair maid, I'll do you a good turn for this some day."

Well, the day was spent, and she got lodging at a lonely house, where there was no one but a woman with hair on her chin, and very long teeth, and her daughter that had the same sort of teeth, but no beard as yet. They gave her some mouldy bread and some small beer for supper, and next day when she was going off, they said there was no one else living in that underground country, and so she might as well live with themselves. "I'll give you food and clothes," said the old woman, "and your choice of three caskets when you are leaving me, and one of them contains more gold and silver and precious stones than the king of England has in his court."

The first task she gave her was to go milk the cows,

but when she went into the byre where they stood, they *lued*, and they kicked, and they horned, so that she was afraid to come near them. But a flight of sparrows came in, and lighted on their heads, and took hold of their ears, and they stood as quiet as lambs till they were milked. Then they all chirruped, "This is what we do for rewarding of you, fair maiden, fair maiden, for giving us crumbs, for giving us crumbs." Then they all flew off, and very sour looks she got from the two women inside for getting away with her life from the cows. "It was not from your own breast you sucked your knowledge," said the young one.

The next morning said the old witch, "Take this short black hank of thread and this long white hank to the stream, and bring the black one back to me white, and the white one black, or you'll sup sorrow." The poor girl took the hanks with a heavy heart and went to the spring, and washed and cried till she was weary, and then sat down on a stone, and wrung her hands. Who should come up at the moment but the poor woman she fed the day she cleared the oven, and she did no more than swale the white hank with the stream, and the black hank against the stream, and the colours were changed in a moment. "This is the good turn I promised you, fair maiden," said she, and she vanished.

As vexed as the witches were before, they were twice as much vexed now, and their faces were fiery and vinegary enough to frighten a horse from his fodder. "Wait till to-morrow!" said they to themselves.

When the breakfast of mouldy bread and small beer was over, said the old hag, "Take that sieve to the stream, and bring it back full of water; there mustn't be a drop wanting." So she went and tried to fill it, and it was no sooner full than it was empty, and she began to cry. Oh, where are my sparrows and my fairy now?" said she. "Here we are," said the birds.

> "Stuff with moss,
>   Plaster with clay,
> And carry it full
>   Of water away."

She did so, and took home the sieve full to the brim. "Oh, ho;" said the angry old witch, "you're too clever for us, I see. Go up to that loft, and take your choice of three caskets you'll find on the table." She went up, and there were three caskets—one of gold, one of silver, and one of lead. She was in doubt which to select, till she heard the sparrows twittering on the roof at the skylight, "Pass by the gold, pass by the silver, but take up the lead, fair maiden." So she did, but as she was quitting the house the old witch was so vexed at her choice, that she snapped up a burning log, and flung it after her.

She ran away very swiftly and as swift came the witches after her, till she came up to where the cow was standing. "Come under me," says the cow; "I'll hide you behind my elder, and I'll put a charm on their eyes. "Did you see a young girl pass this way?" said they. "Yes," said the cow, "she turned into that wood on the left." Off they ran that way, and the cow licked the maiden, and off she ran. Well, when she came near the ram, she heard the clatter of their feet behind her. "Get under that heap of wool," says he, "and they won't see you." "Ram, ram, did you see a young girl run by?" "Yes, I did. She ran into that wood on the right." Off with them again, and the maiden thanked the ram, and ran on. Just as she was near the apple tree, she heard the clatter of their feet again. "Get under the heap of apples," said the tree, and so she did. "Apple tree, apple tree, did you see a young maid run this way?" "Yes, I did. She is hiding in my branches." Up they both climbed, and off ran the maid. They thought to get down and pursue her, but the branches twisted round them and held them fast, and it wasn't till the maid was near the hedge that they were again on land. Just as she was at the hedge, she heard the clatter of their feet, but the fence opened a gap for her, and she was soon in the green meadow where she first opened her eyes in the underground world. When the hags attempted to cross the hedge it pricked them with thorns and brambles, and just as they were over, it tumbled on them, and it took them half a day to get clear again.

A heaviness came over the maid as she sat down to rest

on a green ridge, and when she woke she found herself sitting by the well in the upper world. Her father was glad to see her again, but the wicked women of the family drove her to an out-house to take her meals and sleep. Well, she swept it out, and brushed the cobwebs off the walls, and then she sat down at a little table they gave her, and opened her box to see what was inside. All the silk, and gold, and silver, and jewels that were in it were enough to dazzle anyone's eyes, and she began to hang the walls with the silk curtains, and cover the floor with the fine carpets, that grew in size according as they were wanted, and then she was like a queen in her bower, with as much gold, and silver, and jewels in her casket as she chose.

Oh, weren't the step-mother and her daughter in a bad way when they came by chance into the room! They asked how she got all the fine things, and when she told them, the daughter popped herself head foremost into the well, and there she met all the same adventures as her sister, but she was cross and impudent with every one, and she had no one to help her milking the wicked cows, nor dyeing the hanks, nor filling the sieve, and at last she chose the gold casket, and when the hags sent her away after half starving her, the ram and the cow pucked her with their horns, and the apple tree had like to kill her with the load of fruit it let fall on her, and the hedge wounded her with its thorny boughs, and when she found herself by the well in the upper world she was more dead than alive. It was worse when she came home, and the gold casket was opened, for out there swarmed toads, and frogs, and snakes, that crept under the beds, and filled every corner of the house; and day after day new ones were coming out, and making a purgatory on earth for herself and her mother. The father was glad enough to be let live with his daughter, and there was so much talk about it in the country that the young king came to see the maiden. To make a long story short, they were married, and if they didn't live happy ever after, it surely wasn't the fault of the young queen.

JACK THE CUNNING THIEF.

THERE was a poor farmer who had three sons, and on the same day the three boys went to seek their fortune. The eldest two were sensible, industrious young men; the youngest never did much at home that was any use. He loved to be setting snares for rabbits, and tracing hares in the snow, and inventing all sorts of funny tricks to annoy people at first and then set them laughing.

The three parted at a cross-roads, and Jack took the lonesomest. The day turned out rainy, and he was wet and weary, you may depend, at nightfall, when he came to a lonesome house a little off the road. "What do you want?" says a blear-eyed old woman, that was sitting at the fire. "My supper and a bed to be sure," said he. "You can't get it," said she. "What's to hinder me?" said he. "The owners of the house is," said she, "six honest men that does be out mostly till three or four o'clock in the morning, and if they find you here they'll skin you alive at the very least." "Well, I think," said Jack, "that their very most couldn't be much worse. Come, give me something out of the cupboard, for here I'll stay. Skinning is not much worse than catching your death of cold in a ditch or under a tree such a night as this."

Begonies she got afraid, and gave him a good supper, and when he was going to bed he said if she let any of the six honest men disturb him when they came home she'd sup sorrow for it. When he woke in the morning, there were six ugly-looking spalpeens standing round his bed. He leaned on his elbow, and looked at them with great contempt. "Who are you," said the chief, "and what's your business?" "My name," says he, "is *An Ceann Ghoduidhe* (pr. *Caun Godhy*, Master Thief), and my business just now is to find apprentices and workmen. If I find yous any good, maybe I'll give you a few lessons." Bedad they were a little cowed, and says the head man, "Well, get up, and after breakfast, we'll see who is to be the master, and who the journeyman."

They were just done breakfast, when what should they see but a farmer driving a fine large goat to market. "Will any of you," says Jack, "undertake to steal that goat from the owner before he gets out of the wood, and that without the smallest violence?" "I couldn't do it," says one, and "I couldn't do it," says another. "I'm your master," says Jack, "and I'll do it."

He slipped out, went through the trees to where there was a bend in the road, and laid down his right brogue in the very middle of it. Then he ran on to another bend, and laid down his left brogue and went and hid himself. When the farmer sees the first brogue, he says to himself, "That would be worth something if it had the fellow, but it is worth nothing by itself." He goes on till he comes to the second brogue. "What a fool I was," says he, "not to pick up the other! I'll go back for it." So he tied the goat to a sapling in the hedge, and returned for the brogue. But Jack, who was behind a tree, had it already on his foot, and when the man was beyond the bend he picked up the other and loosened the goat, and led him off through the wood.

Ochone! the poor man couldn't find the first brogue, and when he came back he couldn't find the second, nor neither his goat. "*Mílé* (pr. *millia*) *mollacht!*" says he, "what will I do after promising *Shevaun* (*Siobhan*, Johanna) to buy her a shawl. I must only go and drive another beast to the market unknownst. I'd never hear the last of it if Joan found out what a fool I made of myself."

The thieves were in great admiration at Jack, and wanted him to tell them how he done the farmer, but he wouldn't tell them. By and by, they see the poor man driving a fine fat wether the same way. "Who'll steal that wether," says Jack, "before it's out of the wood, and no roughness used?" "I couldn't" says one, and "I couldn't," says another. "I'll try," says Jack. "Give me a good rope."

The poor farmer was jogging along and thinking of his misfortune, when he sees a man hanging from the bough of a tree. "Lord save us!" says he, "the corpse wasn't there an hour ago." He went on about half a quarter of a mile, and there was another corpse again hanging over the road. "God between us and harm," said he, "am I in my right senses?" There was another turn about the same distance, and just beyond it the third corpse was hanging. "Oh, murdher!" said he; "I'm beside myself. What would bring three hung men so near one another? I must be mad. I'll go back and see if the others are there still."

He tied the wether to a sapling, and back he went. But when he was round the bend, down came the corpse, and loosened the wether, and drove it home through the wood to the robbers' house. You all may think how the poor farmer felt when he could find no one dead or alive going or coming, nor his wether, nor the rope that fastened him. "Oh, misfortunate day!" cried he, "what'll Shevaun say to me now? my morning gone, and the goat and wether lost! I must sell something to make the price of the shawl. Well, the fat bullock is in the nearest field. She won't see me taking it."

Well, if the robbers were not surprised when Jack came into the bawn with the wether. "If you do another trick like this," said the captain, "I'll resign the command to you."

They soon saw the farmer going by again, driving a fat bullock this time. "Who'll bring that fat bullock here," says Jack, "and use no violence?" "I could'nt," says one and "I couldn't," says another. "I'll try," says Jack, and into the wood with him. The farmer was about the spot where he saw the first brogue, when he heard the bleating of a goat off at his right in the wood.

He cocked his ears, and the next thing he heard was the maaing of a sheep. "Blood alive!" says he, "maybe these are my own that I lost." There was more bleating and more maaing. "There they are as sure as a gun," says he, and he tied his bullock to a sapling that grew in the hedge, and into the wood with him. When he got near the place where the cries came from, he heard them a little before him and on he followed them. At last, when he was about half a mile from the spot where he tied the beast, the cries stopped altogether. After searching and searching till he was tired, he returned for his bullock; but there wasn't the ghost of a bullock there nor any where else that he searched.

This time, when the thieves saw Jack and his prize coming into the bawn they couldn't help shouting out, " Jack must be our chief." So there was nothing but feasting and drinking hand to fist the rest of the day. Before they went to bed, they showed Jack the cave where their money was hid, and all their disguises in another cave, and swore obedience to him.

One morning when they were at breakfast, about a week after, said they to Jack, " Will you mind the house for us to-day while we are at the fair of Mochurry ? We hadn't a spree for ever so long : you must get your turn whenever you like." ." Never say't twice," says Jack, and off they went. After they were gone says Jack to the wicked housekeeper, " Do these fellows ever make you a present?" "Ah catch them at it ! indeed an' they don't, purshuin to 'em." "Well, come along with me, and I'll make you a rich woman." He took her to the treasure cave; and while she was in raptures, gazing at the heaps of gold and silver, Jack filled his pockets as full as they could hold, put more into a little bag, and walked out, locking the door on the old hag, and leaving the key in the lock. He then put on a rich suit of clothes, took the goat, and the wether, and the bullock, and drove them before him to the farmer's house.

Joan and her husband were at the door; and when they saw the animals, they clapped their hands and laughed for joy. "Do you know who owns them bastes, neighbours?" "Maybe we don't! sure they're ours." "I found them straying in the wood. Is that bag with ten guineas in it that's hung round the goat's neck yours?" "Faith it isn't." "Well, you may as well keep it for a Godsend; I don't want it. *Banacht llath.*" "Heavens be in your road, good gentleman !"

Jack travelled on till he came to his father's house in the dusk of the evening. He went in. "God save all here !" "God save you kindly, sir !" "Could I have a night's lodging here !" "Oh, sir, our place isn't fit for the likes of a gentleman such as you." "Oh, *musha*, don't yous know your own son ?" Well they opened their eyes, and it was only a strife to see who'd have him in their arms first. " But, Jack asthore, where did you get the fine clothes ?" Oh, you may as well ask me where I got all that money ?" said he, emptying his pockets on the table. Well, they got in a great fright, but when he told them his adventures, they were easier in mind, and all went to bed in great content.

"Father," says Jack, next morning, "Go over to the landlord, and tell him I wish to be married to his daughter." "Faith, I'm afraid he'd only set the dogs at me. If he asks me how you made your money, what'll I say?" "Tell him I am a master thief, and that there is no one equal to me in the three kingdoms; that I am worth a thousand pounds, and all taken from the biggest rogues unhanged. Speak to him when the young lady is by." "It's a droll message you're sending me on: I'm afraid it won't end well." The old man came back in two hours. "Well, what news?" "Droll news enough. The lady didn't seem a bit unwilling: I suppose it's not the first time you spoke to her, and the squire laughed, and said for you to steal the goose off o' the spit in his kitchen next Sunday, and he'd see about it." "O! that won't be hard, any way."

Next Sunday, after the people came from early mass, the squire and all his people were in the kitchen and the goose turning before the fire. The kitchen door opened, and a miserable old beggarman with a big wallet on his back put in his head. "Would the mistress have anything for me when dinner is over, your honour?" "To be sure. We have no room here for you just now; sit in the porch for a while." "God bless your honour's family and yourself!" Soon some one that was sitting near the window cried out, "Oh, sir, there's a big hare scampering like the divel round the bawn. Will we run out and pin him?" "Pin a hare indeed! much chance you'd have; sit where you are." That hare made his escape into the garden, but Jack that was in the beggar's clothes soon let another out of the bag. "Oh, master, there he is still pegging round. He can't make his escape: let us have a chase. The hall door is locked on the inside and Mr. Jack can't get in." "Stay quiet, I tell you." In a few minutes he shouted out again that the hare was there still, but it was the third that Jack was just after giving its liberty. Well, by the laws, they couldn't be kept in any longer. Out pegged every mother's son of 'em, and the squire after them. "Will I turn the spit, your honour, while they're catching the *hareyeen?*" says the beggar. "Do, and don't let anyone in for your life." "Faith an' I won't, you may depend on it." The third hare got away after the others, and when they all came back from the hunt, there was neither beggar nor goose in the kitchen. "Purshuin' to you, Jack," says the landlord, "you've come over me this time."

Well, while they were thinking of making out another dinner, a messenger came from Jack's father to beg that the squire, and the mistress, and the young lady would step across the fields, and take share of what God sent. There was no dirty mean pride about the family, and they walked over, and got a dinner with roast turkey, and roast beef, and their own roast goose, and the squire had like to burst his waistcoat laughing at the trick, and Jack's good clothes and good manners did not take away any liking the young lady had for him already.

While they were taking their punch at the old oak table in the nice clean little parlour with the sanded floor, says the squire, "You can't be sure of my daughter, Jack, unless you steal away my six horses from under the six men that will be watching them to-morrow night in the stable." "I'd do more than that," says Jack, "for a pleasant look from the young lady;" and the young lady's cheeks turned as red as fire.

Monday night the six horses were in their stalls, and a man on every horse, and a good glass of whiskey under every man's waistcoat, and the door was left wide open for Jack. They were merry enough for a long time, and joked and sung, and were pitying the poor fellow, but the small hours crept on, and the whiskey lost its power, and they began to shiver and wish it was morning. A miserable old colliach, with half a dozen bags round her, and a beard half an inch long on her chin, came to the door. "Ah then, tendher-hearted christians," says she, "would you let me in, and allow me a wisp of straw in the corner; the life will be froze out of me if you don't give me shelter." Well, they didn't see any harm in that, and she made herself as snug as she could, and they soon saw her pull out a big black bottle, and take a sup. She coughed and smacked her lips, and seemed a little more comfortable, and the men couldn't take their eyes off her. "Gorsoons," says she, "I'd offer you a drop of this, only you might think it too free-making." "Oh, hang all impedent pride," says one, "we'll take it, and thankee." So she gave them the bottle, and they passed it round, and the last man had the manners to leave half a glass in the bottom for the old woman. They all thanked her, and said it was the best drop ever passed their tongues. "In throth, agras," said she, "it's myself that's glad to show how I value your kindness in giving me shelter; I'm not without another *buideal*, and yous may pass it round while myself finishes what the dasent man left me."

Well, what they drank out of the other bottle only gave them a relish for more, and by the time the last man got to the bottom, the first man was dead asleep in the saddle, for the second bottle had a sleepy posset mixed with the whiskey. The beggar-woman lifted each man down, and laid him in the manger, or under the manger, snug and sausty, drew a stocking over every horse's hoof, and led them away without any noise to one of Jack's father's out-houses. The first thing the squire saw next morning was Jack riding up the avenue, and five horses stepping after the one he rode. "Confound you, Jack!" says he, "and confound the numsculls that let you outwit them?" He went out to the stable, and didn't the poor fellows look very lewd o' themselves, when they could be woke up in earnest!

"After all," says the squire, when they were sitting at breakfast, "it was no great thing to outwit such ninnyhammers. I'll be riding out on the common from one to three to-day, and if you can outwit me of the beast I'll be riding, I'll say you deserve to be my son-in-law." "I'd do more than that," says Jack, "for the honour, if there was no love at all in the matter," and the young lady held up her saucer before her face.

Well, the squire kept riding about and riding about till he was tired, and no sign of Jack. He was thinking of going home at last, when what should he see but one of his servants running from the house as if he was mad. "Oh masther, masther," says he, "as far as he could be heard, "fly home if you wish to see the poor mistress alive! I'm running for the surgeon. She fell down two flights of stairs, and her neck, or her hip, or both her arms are broke, and she's speechless, and it's a mercy if you find the breath in her. Fly as fast as the baste will carry you." "But hadn't you better take the horse? it's a mile and a half to the surgeon's." "Oh, anything you like, master. Oh, *Vuya*, *Vuya*! misthress *alanna*, that I should ever see the day! and your purty body disfigured as it is!" "Here, stop your noise, and be off like wildfire! Oh, my darling, my darling, isn't this a trial!"

He tore home like a fury, and wondered to see no stir outside, and when he flew into the hall, and from that to the parlour, his wife and daughter that were sewing at the table screeched out at the rush he made, and the wild look that was on his face. "Oh, my darling!" said he, when he could speak, "how's this? are you hurt? didn't you fall down the stairs? What happened at all? tell me!" "Why, nothing at all happened, thank God, since you rode out: where did you leave the horse?" Well, no one could describe the state he was in for about quarter of an hour, between joy for his wife and anger with Jack, and *sharoose* for being tricked. He saw the beast soon coming up the avenue, and a little gorsoon in the saddle with his feet in the stirrup leathers. The servant didn't make his appearance for a week, but what did he care with Jack's ten golden guineas in his pocket.

Jack didn't show his nose till next morning, and it was a queer reception he met. "That was all foul play you gave," says the squire. "I'll never forgive you for the shock you gave me. But then I am so happy ever since, that I think I'll give you only one trial more. If you will take away the sheet from under my wife and myself to-night, the marriage may take place to-morrow." "We'll try," says Jack, "but if you keep my bride from me any longer, I'll steal her away if she was minded by fiery dragons."

When the squire and his wife were in bed, and the moon shining in through the window, he saw a head rising over the sill to have a peep, and then bobbing down again. "That's Jack," says the squire: "I'll astonish him a bit," says the squire, pointing a gun at the lower pane. "Oh Lord, my dear!" says the wife, "sure you wouldn't shoot the brave fellow!" "Indeed, an' I wouldn't for a kingdom; there's nothing but powder in it." Up went the head, bang went the gun, down dropped the body, and a great souse was heard on the gravel walk. "Oh Lord," says the lady, "poor Jack is killed or disabled for life." "I hope not," says the squire, and down the stairs he ran. He never minded to shut the door, but opened the gate and ran into the garden. His wife heard his voice at the room door, before he could be under the window and back, as she thought. "Wife, wife!" says he from the door, "the sheet, the sheet! He is not killed, I hope, but he is bleeding like a pig. I must wipe it away as well as I can, and get some one to carry him in with me." She pulled it off the bed and threw it to him. Down he ran like lightning, and he had hardly time to be in the garden, when he was back, and this time he came in in his shirt as he went out.

"High hanging to you, Jack," says he, "for an arrant rogue!" "Arrant rogue?" says she, "Isn't the poor fellow all cut and bruised?" "I didn't much care if he was. What do you think was bobbing up and down at the window, and sossed down so heavy on the walk? a man's clothes stuffed with straw and a couple of stones." "And what did you want with the sheet just now, to wipe his blood if he was only a man of straw?" "Sheet, woman! I wanted no sheet." "Well; whether you wanted it or not, I threw it to you, and you standing outside o' the door." "Oh, Jack, Jack, you terrible tinker!" says the squire, "there's no use in striving with you. We must do without the sheet for one night. We'll have the marriage tomorrow to get ourselves out of trouble."

So married they were, and Jack turned out a real good husband. And the squire and his lady were never tired of praising their son-in-law, "Jack the Cunning Thief."

THE GREEK PRINCESS AND THE YOUNG GARDENER.

THERE was once a king, but I didn't hear what country he was over, and he had one very beautiful daughter. Well he was getting old and sickly, and the doctors found out that the finest medicine in the world for him was the apples of a tree that grew in the orchard just under his window. So you may be sure he had the tree well minded, and used to get the apples counted from the time they were the size of small *marvels*. One harvest, just as they were beginning to turn ripe, the king was awoke one night by the flapping of wings outside in the orchard; and when he looked out, what did he see but a bird among the branches of his tree. Its feathers were so bright they made a light all round them, and the *minute* (moment) it saw the king in his night-cap and night-shirt it picked off an apple, and flew away. "Oh, tattheration to that thief of a gardener!" says he, "this is a nice way he's watching my precious fruit."

He didn't sleep a wink the rest of the night; and as soon as anyone was stirring in the palace, he sent for the gardener, and abused him for his neglect. "Please your majesty!" says he "not another apple you shall lose. My three sons are the best shots at the *bow-arra* in the kingdom, and they and myself will watch in turn every night."

When the night came, the gardener's eldest son took his post in the garden, with his bow strung, and his arrow between his fingers, and watched, and watched. But at the dead hour the king, that was wide awake, heard the flapping of wings, and ran to the window. There was the bright bird in the tree, and the boy fast asleep, sitting with his back to the wall, and his bow on his lap. "Rise, you lazy thief!" says the king, "there's the bird again, tattheration to her!" Up jumped the poor fellow; but while he was fumbling with the arrow and the string, away was the bird with the nicest apple on the tree. Well, to be sure, how the king fumed and fretted, and how he abused the gardener and the boy, and what a twenty-four hours he spent till midnight came again!

He had his eye this time on the second son of the

gardener; but though he was up and lively enough when the clock began to strike twelve, it wasn't done with the last bang when he saw him stretched like one dead on the long grass, and saw the bright bird again, and heard the flap of her wings, and saw her carry away the third apple. The poor fellow woke with the roar the king let at him, and even was time enough to let fly an arrow after the bird. He did not hit her, you may depend; and though the king was mad enough, he saw the poor fellows were under *pishrogues*, and could not help it.

Well, he had some hopes out of the youngest, for he was a brave, active young fellow, that had everybody's good word. There he was ready, and there was the king watching him, and talking to him at the first stroke of twelve. At the last clang, the brightness coming before the bird lighted up the wall and the trees, and the rushing of the wings was heard as it flew into the branches; but at the same instant the crack of the arrow on her side might be heard a quarter of a mile off. Down came the arrow and a large bright feather along with it, and away was the bird, with a screech that was enough to break the drum of your ear. She hadn't time to carry off an apple; and bedad, when the feather was thrown up into the king's room it was heavier than lead, and turned out to be the finest beaten gold.

Well, there was great *cooramuch* made about the youngest boy next day, and he watched night after night for a week, but not a smite of a bird or bird's feather was to be seen, and then the king told him to go home and sleep. Every one admired the beauty of the gold feather *beyant* anything, but the king was fairly bewitched. He was turning it round and round, and rubbing it again' his forehead and his nose the live-long day; and at last he proclaimed that he'd give his daughter and half his kingdom to whoever would bring him the bird with the gold feathers, dead or alive.

The gardener's eldest son had great consate out of himself, and away he set to try for the bird. In the afternoon he sat down under a tree to rest himself, and eat a bit of bread and cold meat that he had in his wallet, when up comes as fine a looking fox as you'd see in the burrow of

Munfin. "Musha, sir," says he, "would you spare a bit of that meat to a poor body that's hungry?" "Well," says the other, "you must have the divel's own assurance, you common robber, to ask me such a question. Here's the answer," and he let fly at the *moddhereen rua*. The arrow scraped from his side up over his back, as if he was made of hammered iron, and stuck in a tree a couple of perches off. "Foul play," says the fox; "but I respect your young brother, and will give you a bit of advice. At nightfall you'll come into a village. One side of the street you'll see a large room lighted up, and filled with young men and women, dancing and drinking. The other side you'll see a house with no light, only from the fire in the front room, and no one near it but a man, and his wife, and their child. Take a fool's advice, and get lodging there." With that he curled his tail over his crupper, and trotted off.

The boy found things as the fox said, but *begonies* he chose the dancing and drinking, and there we'll leave him. In a week's time, when they got tired at home waiting for him, the second son said he'd try his fortune, and off he set. He was just as ill-natured and foolish as his brother, and the same thing happened to him. Well, when a week was over, away went the youngest of all, and as sure as the hearth-money, he sat under the same tree, and pulled out his bread and meat, and the same fox came up and saluted him. Well, the young fellow shared his dinner with the *moddhereen*, and he wasn't long beating about the bush, but told the other he knew all about his business. "I'll help you," says he, "if I find you're biddable. So just at nightfall you'll come into a village, ... Good-bye till to-morrow." It was just as the fox said, but the boy took care not to go near dancer, drinker, fiddler, or piper. He got welcome in the quiet house to supper and bed, and was on his journey next morning before the sun was the height of the trees.

He wasn't gone a quarter of a mile when he saw the fox coming out of a wood that was by the road-side. "Good morrow, fox," says one; "Good morrow, sir," says the other. "Have you any notion how far you have to travel till you find the golden bird?" "Dickens a notion have I;—how could I ?" "Well, I have. She's in the King of Spain's palace, and that's a good two hundred miles off." "Oh, dear! we'll be a week going." "No we won't. Sit down on my tail, and we'll soon make the road short." "Tail indeed! that 'ud be the droll saddle, my poor *moddhereen*." "Do as I tell you, or I'll leave you to yourself." Well, rather than vex him he sat down on the tail that was spread out level like a wing, and away they went like thought. They overtook the wind that was before them, and the wind that came after didn't overtake them. In the afternoon, they stopped in a wood near the King of Spain's palace, and there they staid till night-fall.

"Now," says the fox, "I'll go before you to make the minds of the guards easy, and you'll have nothing to do but go from one lighted hall to another lighted hall till you find the golden bird in the last. If you have a head on you, you'll bring himself and his cage outside the door, and no one then can lay hands on him or you. If you haven't a head I can't help you, nor no one else." So he went over to the gates.

In a quarter of an hour the boy followed, and in the first hall he passed he saw a score of armed guards standing upright, but all dead asleep. In the next he saw a dozen, and in the next half a dozen, and in the next three, and in the room beyond that there was no guard at all, nor lamp, nor candle, but it was as bright as day; for there was the golden bird in a common wood and wire cage, and on the table were the three apples turned into solid gold.

On the same table was the most lovely golden cage eye ever beheld, and it entered the boy's head that it would be a thousand pities not to put the precious bird into it, the common cage was so unfit for her. Maybe he thought of the money it was worth; any how he made the exchange, and he had soon good reason to be sorry for it. The instant the shoulder of the bird's wing touched the golden wires, he let such a *squawk* out of him as was enough to break all the panes of glass in the windows, and at the same minute the three men, and the half dozen, and the dozen, and the score men, woke up and clattered their swords and spears, and surrounded the poor boy, and jibed, and cursed, and swore at him, till he didn't know whether it's his foot or head he was standing on. They called the king, and told him what happened, and he put on a very grim face. "It's on a gibbet you ought to be this moment," says he, "but I'll give you a chance of your life, and of the golden bird too. I lay you under prohibitions, and restrictions, and death, and destruction, to go and bring me the King of *Morōco's* bay filly that outruns the wind, and leaps over the walls of castle-bawns. When you fetch her into the bawn of this palace, you must get the golden bird, and liberty to go where you please."

Out passed the boy, very down-hearted, but as he went along, who should come out of a brake but the fox again!

"Ah, my friend," says he, "I was right when I suspected you hadn't a head on you; but I won't rub your hair again' the grain. Get on my tail again, and when we come to the king of Morōco's palace we'll see what we can do." So away they went like thought. The wind, &c., &c., &c.

Well, the nightfall came on them in a wood near the palace, and says the fox, "I'll go and make things easy for you at the stables, and when you are leading out the filly, don't let her touch the door, nor door-posts, nor anything but the ground, and that with her hoofs; and if you haven't a head on you once you are in the stable, you'll be worse off than before."

So the boy delayed for a quarter of an hour, and then he went into the big bawn of the palace. There were two rows of armed men reaching from the gate to the stable, and every man was in the depth of deep sleep, and through them with the boy till he got into the stable. There was the filly, as handsome a beast as ever stretched leg, and there was one stable boy with a currycomb in his hand, and another with a bridle, and another with a sieve of oats, and another with an armfull of hay, and all as if they were cut out of stone. The filly was the only live thing in the place except himself. She had a common wood and leather saddle on her back, but a golden saddle with the nicest work on it was hung from the post, and he thought it the greatest pity not to put it in place of the other. Well, I believe there was some *pishrogues* over it for a saddle; any how he took off the other, and put the gold one in its place.

Out came a squeel from the filly's throat when she felt the strange article, that might be heard from Tombrick to Bunclody, and all as ready were the armed men and the stable boys to run and surround the *omadhan* of a boy, and the king of Moroco was soon there along with the rest, with a face on him as black as the sole of your foot. After he stood enjoying the abuse the poor boy got from everybody for some time, he says to him, "You deserve high hanging for your *impedence*, but I'll give you a chance for your life and the filly too. I lay on you all sorts of prohibitions, and restrictions, and death, and destruction to go bring me Princess Golden Locks, the King of Greek's daughter. When you deliver her into my hand, you may have the 'daughter of the wind,' and welcome. Come in and take your supper and your rest, and be off at the flight of night."

The poor boy was down in the mouth, you may suppose, as he was walking away next morning, and very much ashamed when the fox looked up in his face after coming out of the wood. "What a thing it is," says he, "not to have a head when a body wants it worst; and here we have a fine long journey before us to the king of Greek's palace. The worse luck now, the same always. Here, get on my tail, and we'll be making the road shorter." So he sat on the fox's tail, and swift as thought they went. The wind that, &c., &c., &c., and in the evening they were eating their bread and cold meat in the wood near the castle.

"Now," says the fox, when they were done, "I'll go before you to make things easy. Follow me in a quarter of an hour. Don't let Princess Golden Locks touch the jambs of the doors with her hands, or hair, or clothes, and if you're asked any favour, mind how you answer. Once she's outside the door, no one can take her from you." Into the palace walked the boy at the proper time, and there were the score, and the dozen, and the half dozen, and the three guards all standing up or leaning on their arms, and all dead asleep, and in the farthest room of all was the Princess Golden Locks, as lovely as Venus herelf. She was asleep in one chair, and her father, the King of Greek, in another. He stood before her for ever so long, with the love sinking deeper into his heart every minute, till at last he went down on one knee, and took her darling white hand in his hand, and kissed it.

When she opened her eyes, she was a little frightened, but I believe not very angry, for the boy, as I call him, was a fine handsome young fellow, and all the respect and love that ever you could think of was in his face. She asked him what he wanted, and he stammered, and blushed, and began his story six times, before she understood it. "And would you give me up to that ugly black king of Morōco?" says she. "I am obliged to do so," says he, "by prohibitions, and restrictions, and death, and destruction, but I'll have his life and free you, or lose my own. If I can't get you for my wife, my days on the earth will be short." "Well," says she, "let me take leave of my father at any rate." "Ah, I can't do that," says he, "or they'd all waken, and myself would be put to death, or sent to some task worse than any I got yet." But she asked leave at any rate to kiss the old man;—that wouldn't waken him, and then she'd go. How could he refuse her, and his heart tied up in every curl of her hair? But, bedad, the moment her lips touched her father's, he let a cry, and every one of the score, the dozen . . . . guards woke up, and clashed their arms, and were going to make *gibbets* of the foolish boy.

But the king ordered them to hold their hands, till he'd be *insensed* of what it was all about, and when he heard the boy's story he gave him a chance for his life. "There is," says he, "a great heap of clay in front of the palace, that won't let the sun shine on the walls in the middle of summer. Every one that ever worked at it found two shovelfulls added to it for every one they threw away. Remove it, and I'll let my daughter go with you. If you're the man I suspect you to be, I think she'll be in no danger of being wife to that yellow *Molott*."

Early next morning was the boy tackled to his work, and for every shovelfull he flung away two came back on him, and at last he could hardly get out of the heap that gathered round him. Well, the poor fellow scrambled out some way, and sat down on a sod, and he'd have cried only for the shame of it. He began at it in ever so many places, and one was still worse than the other, and in the heel of the evening, when he was sitting with his head between his hands, who should be standing before him but the fox? "Well, my poor fellow," says he, "you're low enough. Go in: I won't say anything to add to your trouble. Take your supper and your rest: to-morrow will be a new day."

"How is the work going off," says the king when they were at supper. "Faith, your Majesty," says the poor boy, "it's not going off, but coming on it is. I suppose you'll have the trouble of digging me out at sunset to-morrow, and waking me." "I hope not," says the princess with a smile on her kind face, and the boy was as happy as anything the rest of the evening.

He was wakened up next morning with voices shouting, and bugles blowing, and drums beating, and such a hullibulloo he never heard in his life before. He ran out to see what was the matter, and there, where the heap of clay was the evening before, were soldiers, and servants, and lords, and ladies, dancing like mad for joy that it was gone. "Ah, my poor fox!" says he to himself, "this is your work." Well there was little delay about his return. The King was going to send a great retinue with the princess and himself, but he wouldn't let him take the trouble. "I have a friend," says he, "that will bring us both to the King of Morōco's palace in a day, d— fly away with him!"

There was great crying when she was parting from her father. "Ah!" says he, "what a lonesome life I'll have now! Your poor brother in the power of that wicked witch, and kept away from us, and now you taken from me in my old age!" Well, while they both were walking on through the wood, and he telling her how much he loved her, out walked the fox from behind a brake, and in a short time he and she were sitting on the brush, and holding one another fast for fear of slipping off, and away they went like thought. The wind, &c., &c., and in the evening he and she were in the big bawn of the King of Morōco's castle.

ell," says he to the boy, "you done your duty well;
out the bay filly. I'd give the full of the bawn of
fillies, if I had them, for this handsome princess. Get
ur steed, and here is a good purse of guineas for the
"Thank you," says he. "I suppose you'll let me
hands with the princess before I start." "Yes, in-
and welcome." Well, he was some little time about
ind-shaking, and before it was over he had her fixed
behind him; and while you could count three, he, and
nd the filly were through all the guards, and a hun-
erches away. On they went, and next morning they
n the wood near the King of Spain's palace, and there
ie fox before them. "Leave your princess here with
says he, "and go get the golden bird and the three
. If you don't bring us back the filly along with the
must carry you both home myself."
ll, when the King of Spain saw the boy and the filly
bawn, he made the golden bird, and the golden cage,
ie golden apples be brought out and handed to him,
as very thankful and very glad of his prize. But the
uld not part with the nice beast without petting it,
ibbing it, and while no one was expecting such a
he was up on its back, and through the guards, and
lred perches away, and he wasn't long till he came
he left his princess and the fox.
y hurried away till they were safe out of the King of
s land, and then they went on easier; and if I was to
u all the loving things they said to one another, the
vouldn't be over till morning. When they were pass-
ie village of the dance house, they found his two
rs begging, and they brought them along. When
ame to where the fox appeared first, he begged the
man to cut off his head and his tail. He would not
for him; he shivered at the very thought, but the
brother was ready enough. The head and tail va-
with the blows, and the body changed into the finest
man you could see, and who was he but the princess's
r that was bewitched. Whatever joy they had be-
hey had twice as much now, and when they arrived
palace bonfires were set blazing, oxes roasting, and

puncheons of wine put out in the lawn. The young Prince of Greek was married to the King's daughter, and the prince's sister to the gardener's son. He and she went a shorter way back to her father's house, with many attendants, and the King was so glad of the golden bird and the golden apples, that he sent a wagon full of gold and a wagon full of silver along with them.

THE GIANT AND HIS ROYAL SERVANTS.

THERE was once a very good king and queen that would be as happy as the day was long only they had no children. So as they were one day sitting in a garden chair by the edge of the pond at the bottom of the lawn, and talking how lonesome the palace was for young people, a giant stepped out of the grove that was behind them, and says he, "King and queen, if you'll give me your eldest son when he's twenty-one years of age, I'll give you a necklace, ma'am, and so that you never put it off night or day, you will have four sons and three daughters in the next ten years. I'll be here to-morrow at the same hour to know your will."

They talked and they talked all the rest of that day, and till they went to sleep, but the end was—they'd take the giant's offer:—twenty-two years was a long time off, and many a thing falls out between the milking of the cow and the print of butter coming to the table. They agreed to the giant's offer, and he went away well pleased. In less than a year's time a prince was born, and the queen was not tired till she had her four sons and her three daughters sitting at the table with herself and her husband. They were all as handsome as the sun, moon, and stars, and there was no sorrow till the eldest prince was near his twenty-first birthday.

The very day to the hour, they were sitting in the very same seat when the giant stepped out of the grove, and demanded their eldest born. "I'll wait for him here," said he: "don't keep me long." They went up to the castle and a young man grandly dressed soon came, and appeared before the giant. They talked a little, and the giant then handed him a beautiful little whip. "If I make you a present of that nice whip, what will you do with it.' "Ah, won't I whip away the cats and dogs when they go near the roast and boiled in the kitchen!" "Go back and tell your master and mistress that it is the heir and not the kitchen-boy I want." Another young man came down. "Are you the eldest prince in this palace?" "Yes." "Isn't that a nice whip?" "Ah, isn't it?" "If I give it to you for a present, what will you do with it?" "Won't I whip away the hounds when they want to eat up the fox, brush and all!" "Go and tell your master and mistress that if they don't send me their eldest son and heir, I'll burn down their castle and theirselves and all their children along with it."

The prince came at last, and when he looked in his face he knew it was the man he wanted. They got into a boat, and though the pond was not twenty perches broad, and the boat went as swift as an arrow, they were an hour before they got to the other side, and there the prince found a strange country round him, and the mountain that was fifty miles before them in the morning was now fifty miles behind them. They mounted two horses that were waiting for them, and these went like the wind, and when they were after passing seven mountains, seven glens, and seven moors, they came to the giant's castle on a hill.

They went in, and they got their supper, but the giant took his supper first, and made the prince and a very beautiful young girl wait on him, before they were allowed to get their own. "Now," said he, "the girl will show you to the room where you are to take your rest. She is a king's daughter as well as you are a king's son. A witch foretold that I should be waited on by princes and princesses, and now it's come to pass. I'll tell you in the morning, your work for to-morrow."

When breakfast was over, he took the prince into the bawn. "There," said he, "is a stable that wasn't cleaned for seven years. I am going to look after my flocks and herds; have it so clean when I return at sunset that I may roll a golden apple in at one door, and out at another." Away he went, and to work fell the prince; but for every *sprong*-full he threw out, two came in, and when the princess brought him his dinner, there he was standing outside the door, and the stable as full of litter and dung as it could hold.

A smile came on her face as she saw his sorrowful looks, but she spoke cheerfully. "Come, prince, take the dinner I have cooked for you, and if you don't object I'll join you: we are equal in birth and we are equal in misfortune." He had little appetite, but he was glad of anything that brought himself and the beautiful princess together. So while they were eating, she told him that she was secured in the same manner as himself; that he was the second, and that in some years he'd have scores of servants, all sons and daughters of kings, but that whoever could perform three tasks he'd get would have a chance of escape. "I had a godmother," said she, "who was an enchantress, and I have power that the giant knows nothing about. Look here." She took the sprong, flung out three fulls of it, and all that was in the stable followed it into the great lough at the bottom of the bawn.

Glad enough was the prince, and if he did'nt thank the princess, and make all the loving speeches in the world to her, it's no matter. They didn't feel the time passing till the giant came home, and very bitter he looked when he found the stable cleared. He said not a word all the time they were waiting on him at supper, but when they were ready for bed, he told the prince he had another small job for him in the morning.

Sure enough, the task he put on him the second day was to catch a filly in the paddock. "There is a golden bridle for you," said he, "and if you succeed, that bridle is your own." Away went the giant to look after his flocks and herds, and a sore forenoon the poor prince had, chasing the filly round the paddock, and striving to tempt her with a *boorawn* of oats. But dinner-time came, and there was his dear princess coming over the stile with his dinner. She knew he'd have no appetite in the state he was in, and so the first thing she done after laying down the cloth on the grass, was to take an old jaggedy bridle with a rusty bit out of her pocket, and shake it over her head. As soon as the filly seen it, she run to them capering, and shaking her ears, and stood like a lamb till it was fitted on her. Well, such a dinner, and such loving talk as they had with each other till near sunset, and then she went in, the way the giant wouldn't see them together. As cross as he looked before, he looked ten times crosser now, but he kept in his anger.

Next morning after breakfast, said he to the prince, "There is a tree at the corner of the paddock, and a raven's nest in the branches of it. There are five eggs in the nest, and I want them for my supper to-night. If you break or lose e'er a one of them you needn't expect much good treatment from me. If you bring them safe and sound, I'll marry you to the princess there after supper, and you will live as happy as the day is long."

Well, I think that women aren't so selfish somehow as men. The prince looked glad enough, but there wasn't a morsel of gladness on the princess's face, and so everything went on as usual next morning. The giant went to look after his goats, and sheep, and cattle, the princess readied up the house, and the prince went down to the tree. A wearisome tree it was on him. The body of it was as smooth as that table, and there wasn't a twig sticking out of it for more than a score of feet from the top of the ditch where it grew. He'd grip it with arms and legs till he'd be up about six feet, and then he'd come down with a flop, and after a little rest he'd spit in his palms, and try it again, and down he'd come with a flop once more.

He was worse off to-day when the darling princess came with his dinner than he was the other days, and as much as she pitied him, she couldn't help laughing at the state the legs and arms of his clothes were in. He didn't much enjoy her merriment, but she soon gave him relief. She took from her pocket two magic rods and gave them to him, and told him how to use them, and he was soon climbing the tree like a may-boy. The rods went into the wood like a nail into a cabbage stalk, and then when his left foot was on one he pulled the other out, and stuck it in for his right foot, and so on till he got among the branches. When he came to the nest, he put one egg in his mouth, one in each pocket, and two in the breasts of his coat, and was soon down and eating the happiest dinner he ever tasted.

And says he when the cloth was removed, "What matter, my darling, if the giant keeps us here with him itself when he marries us? Love will make our lives as happy as they can be. Why, I don't wish for anything in the world only to be in your company, and be looking at you, and hearing you speak." "Don't once think, prince," said she, "that I'll be satisfied with such marriage as the giant can put on us, nor to see you and myself and whatever children God would send all his slaves. Don't say a single word when he goes about marrying us. You may be sure I won't open my lips, and when he sends us into the same room, you'll know my intentions better."

It was all as she said, and when the prince and princess were sent by the giant into the room, she pointed out three little images of women, one on the chimney-piece, one on the table, and one on the window-seat. She pricked her finger, and let a drop of blood fall on the mouth of every little image, and then said, "By virtue of my magic power, I charge you to answer the giant's three questions." She then went out through a door that couldn't be noticed from the rest of the wall where it was set. He followed her, and they went down to the stable where the filly was eating its hay. He bridled and saddled the beast, got into his seat, set her behind him, cleared the bawn gate, and to the road with them in the direction of his father's palace.

The giant went to bed, and about nine o'clock, he cried out, "Prince, are you asleep?" "Not yet," was the answer that came from the mantle-piece. At midnight he cried out, "Prince, are you asleep?" "Going asleep," says the image on the table. At one o'clock he cried again, "Prince, are you asleep?" "Dead asleep," says the image on the window-stool. "That's well," says the giant, and himself went off asleep at once.

Next morning he knocked at the door, and knocked, and knocked again, and then he burst it in. There was no one there but the three images, and these he broke in a thousand pieces. He saw the hidden door open, and guessed what happened, and to the road with him. The wind before him he overtook, and the wind after him didn't overtake him. About noon the princess cried out, "I feel the hot breath of the giant at my back; put your hand in the filly's right ear, take out what you'll find, and fling it behind you." He found a twig of wild ash, turned round, and flung it at the giant, who was sweeping down on them like a tempest. Up sprung a tangled wood between them, and the roar the giant let out of him might be heard ten miles off. There they left him, tearing himself through brambles and spikes, and on they flew.

About three hours after, the princess cried out again, "I feel the giant's breath scorching my back: put your hand into the filly's left ear, and fling what you'll find in it at him." He did so, and found a bubble of water. Looking back, there was the giant like a devouring fire racing in on them, but when he threw the bubble at him, a great broad lake appeared where the grass and bushes and stones were a few minutes before, and as fast as the filly went, the water widened after her. In he dashed, and the heat of his body sent the water hissing and sputtering up into the clouds. But he went through it like an eel or a salmon, and just as the sun was setting, the princess cried out once more, "The giant's breath is scorching my back. Alight, and throw this apple as straight as you can at his forehead. Be steady. If you miss we are lost." Down he got, took the apple, and just as the giant was within ten perches of him, he flung it with force and courage. The noise it made on his forehead was like a cannon ball striking a rock. The giant fell like a huge tree and never drew breath again.

They were now at the edge of the wood where the prince's father's palace was built; but when they got to the gatehouse, the princess would not go further. Said she to him, "There is another trial before us. Go you up to the castle, and tell them what you like, and come back for me. But if you kiss anyone, or let anyone kiss you, it is likely we shall never be man and wife." So she staid walking about, and he went up the walk to the hall-door.

I needn't tell you what joy there was before him, and how all his family gathered round him, and hugged him, but thought it mighty queer that he kept his hand on his mouth, and wouldn't let even his mother kiss him. Well, things were getting a little quiet, and he was just beginning to tell about his princess and where she was, when a forward young damsel, that was striving to make him fond of her before the giant took him away, burst through the crowd, and cried, "Oh, is this my betrothed prince that's come back to us?" and bedad, before he could defend himself, she gave him a smack that sounded like the slap of a wet shoe on a flag. The same instant he lost all memory of what happened since the giant took him away, and stood like a fool in the middle of the crowd. Well, a great feast was made, and the forward lady sat by his side, and there was nothing but joy, and in a day or two he was to be married.

After the princess walked about for an hour, she grew very melancholy and said to herself, "Ah, I guessed what would happen, but I'll recover him yet." She asked the gate-keeper's wife would she give her house room for a week or two, and instead of promising to pay her well, she laid down five guineas on the table. They made her welcome, and there she staid, knitting and sewing at the window, and the young gentlemen of the court used often pass by to have a look at her, and the ladies undervalued her beauty, and still they were speaking of her continually at the palace. The prince found himself very much disturbed every time he had a sight of her.

At last the wedding-day came, and they were all after dinner, and about to walk into the chapel to have the marriage celebrated, when the princess came into the hall very nicely dressed, and asked the king if she might make some entertainment for the company. He gave her leave, and she took a nice little cock and hen out of a bag and set them on the table, and threw some oats before them, and the hen began to pick. The cock drove her away, and she cried out, "Ah, prince, is that my reward for cleaning out the stable for you?" The bridegroom did not understand the meaning, and she threw some more oats. The cock drove away the hen again, and again she reminded him of catching the filly and enabling him to climb the tree. At last, when he drove her away the third time, she cried, "Oh you ungrateful prince, is this the way you reward me for shedding my blood for you, and saving your life?" The princess at that moment stretched her hand towards the prince, and when he saw the mark of the cut, he gave a great shout, caught her in his arms, and cried, "You are my lost bride indeed, I'll have no other." His memory was come back to him, and he explained to the company all that happened to him in the giant's house and after, and all the princess did for him. Such hugging and kissing as she got from the king and queen and their children you never heard of, and all the company soon went into the chapel, and the wedding was celebrated.

And indeed the forward bride was so clever with a foolish young lord that she forsook when the prince returned, that he asked leave of the king and queen and the bishop to have a second wedding the same day. "The more the merrier," said they, and the king was glad, as she couldn't go about making a blowing-horn of her disappointment. The princess never again reminded her husband what she ventured for him, and the forward lady never let a day pass without insensing *her* husband how lucky he was to catch herself.

———>◆◆◆<———

THE LAZY BEAUTY AND HER AUNTS.

There was once a poor widow woman, who had a daughter that was as handsome as the day, and as lazy as a pig, saving your presence. The poor mother was the most industrious person in the townland, and was a particularly good hand at the spinning-wheel. It was the wish of her heart that her daughter should be as handy as herself; but she'd get up late, eat her breakfast before she'd finish her prayers, and then go about dawdling, and anything she handled seemed to be burning her fingers. She drawled her words as if it was a great trouble to her to speak, or as if her tongue was as lazy as her body. Many a heart-scald her poor mother got with her, and still she was only improving like dead fowl in August.

Well, one morning that things were as bad as they could be, and the poor woman was giving tongue at the rate of a mill-clapper, who should be riding by but the king's son. "Oh dear, oh dear, good woman!" said he, "you must have a very bad child to make you scold so terribly. Sure it can't be this handsome girl that vexed you!" "Oh, please your Majesty, not at all," says the old dissembler. "I was only checking her for working herself too much. Would your Majesty believe it? She spins three pounds of flax in a day, weaves it into linen the next, and makes it all into shirts the day after." "My gracious," says the prince, "she's the very lady that will just fill my mother's eye, and herself's the greatest spinner in the kingdom. Will you put on your daughter's bonnet and cloak if you please, ma'am, and set her behind me? Why, my mother will be so delighted with her, that perhaps she'll make her her daughter-in-law in a week, that is, if the young woman herself is agreeable."

Well, between the confusion, and the joy, and the fear of being found out, the women didn't know what to do; and before they could make up their minds, young Anty (Anastasia) was set behind the prince, and away he and his attendants went, and a good heavy purse was left behind with the mother. She *pullillued* a long time after all was gone, in dread of something bad happening to the poor girl.

The prince couldn't judge of the girl's breeding or wit from the few answers he pulled out of her. The queen was struck in a heap when she saw a young country girl sitting behind her son, but when she saw her handsome face, and heard all she could do, she didn't think she could make too much of her. The prince took an opportunity of whispering her that if she didn't object to be his wife she must strive to please his mother. Well, the evening went by, and the prince and Anty were getting fonder and fonder of one another, but the thought of the spinning used to send the cold to her heart every moment. When bed-time came, the old queen went along with her to a beautiful bed-room,

...e was bidding her good night, she pointed to ...e flax, and said, "You may begin as soon as ... morrow morning, and I'll expect to see these ...s in nice thread the morning after." Little did ... sleep that night. She kept crying and lament... didn't mind her mother's advice better. When ... alone next morning, she began with a heavy ... hough she had a nice mahogany wheel and the ... you ever saw, the thread was breaking every ...ne while it was as fine as a cobweb, and the ...rse as a little boy's whipcord. At last she ... chair back, let her hands fall in her lap, and ... crying.

...old woman with surprising big feet appeared ...t the same moment, and said, "What ails you, ...ne colleen?" "An' haven't I all that flax to ... to-morrow morning, and I'll never be able to ...ve yards of fine thread of it put together." "An' ... think bad to ask poor *Colliagh Cushmōr* (Old-foot) to your wedding with the young prince? ...ise me that, all your three pounds will be made ...st of thread while you're taking your sleep to-...ndeed you must be there and welcome, and I'll ... all the days of your life." "Very well; stay ...n till tea-time, and tell the queen she may come ...read as early as she likes to-morrow morning." ... she said; and the thread was finer and evener ...t you see with fly-fishers. "My brave girl you ... the queen. I'll get my own mahogany loom ... you, but you needn't do anything more to-day. ... rest, work and rest, is my motto. To-morrow ... all this thread, and who knows what may

... girl was more frightened this time than the last, ... so afraid to lose the prince. She didn't even ...o put the warp in the gears, nor how to use the ... she was sitting in the greatest grief, when a ...u who was mighty well-shouldered about the ... once appeared to her, told her her name was ...*manmōr*, and made the same bargain with her as Colliach Cushmōr. Great was the queen's pleasure when she found early in the morning a web as fine and white as the finest paper you ever saw. "The darling you were!" says she. "Take your ease with the ladies and gentlemen to-day, and if you have all this made into nice shirts to-morrow you may present one of them to my son, and be married to him out of hand."

Oh, wouldn't you pity poor Anty the next day, she was now so near the prince, and, maybe, would be soon so far from him. But she waited as patiently as she could with scissors, needle, and thread in hand, till a minute after noon. Then she was rejoiced to see the third old woman appear. She had a big red nose, and informed Anty that people called her *Shron Mor Rua* on that account. She was up to her as good as the others, for a dozen fine shirts were lying on the table when the queen paid her an early visit.

Now there was nothing talked of but the wedding, and I needn't tell you it was grand. The poor mother was there along with the rest, and at the dinner the old queen could talk of nothing but the lovely shirts, and how happy herself and the bride would be after the honeymoon, spinning, and weaving, and sewing shirts and shifts without end. The bridegroom didn't like the discourse, and the bride liked it less, and he was going to say something, when the footman came up to the head of the table, and said to the bride, "Your ladyship's aunt, Colliach Cushmōr, bade me ask might she come in." The bride blushed and wished she was seven miles under the floor, but well became the prince,—"Tell Mrs. Cushmōr," said he, "that any relation of my bride's will be always heartily welcome wherever she and I are." In came the woman with the big foot, and got a seat near the prince. The old queen didn't like it much, and after a few words she asked rather spitefully, "Dear ma'am, what's the reason your foot is so big?" "*Musha*, faith, your majesty, I was standing almost all my life at the spinning-wheel, and that's the reason." "I declare to you, my darling," said the prince, "I'll never allow you to spend one hour at the same spinning-wheel." The same footman said again, "Your ladyship's aunt, Colliach Cromanmōr, wishes to come in, if the genteels and yourself have no objection." Very *sharoose* (displeased) was Princess Anty, but the prince sent her welcome, and she took her seat, and drank healths apiece to the company. "May I ask, ma'am?" says the old queen, "why you're so wide half way between the head and the feet?" "That, your majesty, is owing to sitting all my life at the loom." "By my sceptre," says the prince, "my wife shall never sit there an hour." The footman again came up. "Your ladyship's aunt, Colliach Shron Mor Rua, is asking leave to come into the banquet." More blushing on the bride's face, but the bridegroom spoke out cordially, "Tell Mrs. Shron Mor Rua she's doing us an honour." In came the old woman, and great respect she got near the top of the table, but the people down low put up their tumblers and glasses to their noses to hide the grins. "Ma'am," says the old queen, "will you tell us, if you please, why your nose is so big and red?" "Throth, your majesty, my head was bent down over the stitching all my life, and all the blood in my body ran into my nose." "My darling," said the prince to Anty, "if ever I see a needle in your hand, I'll run a hundred miles from you."

"And in troth, girls and boys, though it's a diverting story, I don't think the moral is good; and if any of you *thuckeens* go about imitating Anty in her laziness, you'll find it won't thrive with you as it did with her. She was beautiful beyond compare, which none of you are, and she had three powerful fairies to help her besides. There's no fairies now, and no prince or lord to ride by, and catch you idling or working; and maybe, after all, the prince and herself were not so very happy when the cares of the world or old age came on them."

Thus was the tale ended by poor old *Shebale* (Sybilla) Father Murphy's housekeeper, in Coolbawn, Barony of Bantry, about half a century since.

THE GILLA NA GRUAGA DONNA.

THERE was once a boy, and his name was *Gilla na Gruaga Donna* (the fellow with the brown hair), and he had no work to do at home, and little to eat; so he said he'd go look for service. His mother gave him his cake and a good piece of cold bacon in his little bag, and he went on with a light heart, singing like a lark. He sat down in the afternoon by the side of a ditch, to eat a bit of his bread and his meat, and if he did so sure came up an old beggarwoman and asked for some charity. "Faith," said he, "I haven't a halfpenny—brass, gold, or silver about me, but if you don't object to a bit of bread and cold meat, here's a share of what's going." She took what he offered, and prayed all sorts of good prayers for him. At nightfall my poor fellow didn't see a house in sight, and he put up with a bunch of withered grass in a dry ditch.

While he was asleep, he thought a beautiful woman came and stood over him, and said, "Gilla na Gruaga Donna, because you shared the little you had with me, here's a purse with one guinea in it, and every time you take one out, another will come in its place." When he awoke in the morning, and looked about him, he found the same sort of purse he saw in his dream lying by his side, and, better than that, a guinea in it. "This is luck," said he, but he didn't believe that it would be renewed for all that.

However, he came to a town and gave his guinea at the eating house to be changed, and when he was putting his change back, bedad he found another guinea there to keep it company. "This is just what the vision said," says Gilla to himself, and he turned back, and made his family comfortable, and got such a taste for travelling that he set out again. He came to Dublin, and bought fine clothes, and a watch to put in his fob, and a coach-and-six, and drove along to see foreign countries.

As he was rattling along by a king's palace, he happened to look up, and there, at a window, was the finest young princess he ever beheld. So he bade his coachman drive to the gate-house, and sent up his footman to ask leave of the king to see his lawn and his demesne. The king asked the man about his master, but he could only tell he believed he was a great lord going about for his pleasure. He had no end of money, and didn't seem to know what to do with it. So the king sent down word to the gentleman to go about in his lawn and his demense as much as he liked; and while he was driving, who should meet him but the king himself and his daughter, and she in her side-saddle on the back of a *dawney* little pony. "Well, they weren't long getting acquainted. Gilla got out of his coach and walked by the princess's pony; and nothing would do the king but to invite the stranger to come and spend a week or so at the palace.

It wasn't long till Gilla and the princess were as fond of one another as if they were acquainted a hundred years. The king often asked Gilla what rank of life he was born in, but he didn't like to say he was only a poor cottierman's son. One evening when the cunning king found Gilla very comfortable—and no wonder he was comfortable! the princess told him that very day that she'd marry him if her father agreed—made him tipsy, and got out of him that he was only a poor man's son, and that it was a magic purse, that was never without a guinea in it, that put it in his power to travel in state. "Ah, show me this wonderful purse!" said the king; and Gilla was fool enough to do so. The king held it in his hand for a long time, and the next evening they were very merry again. "I am never tired looking at your nice purse," said he; and, indeed, so it appeared, for he kept turning it and re-turning it in his hands for ever so long; and once, when Gilla's eyes were another way, he changed it for one he got made that very day, so like it that scarcely anyone could see the smallest differ.

Next day they were all driving out, and Gilla gave the guinea and change that was left by the cunning king in his purse, away to some poor people. But when he put in his hand again to pay turnpike, or something or other, dickens a guinea or a half-penny was there. Well, he turned all manner of colours, looked at the purse, and was sure it was the same one, and didn't know what in the world to think. When he had an opportunity he told the princesss what happened, and said he'd be obliged to leave the palace. "Oh, what matter!" said she. "Sure, if you are of good blood my father won't mind whether you are poor or rich."

So she went to her father, and told him what happened, but she was sorry enough for what she *done*. The king said it wasn't a nice thing to be on such free terms with a stranger, and bade her go to her own rooms till she heard from him.

When Gilla inquired for the princess next morning, they told him she was on a visit to an aunt that was dying fifty miles away; and when he asked for the king, they told him he was busy at his accounts. "Oh, ho!" said Gilla to himself, "my welcome here is worn out." So he left his best respects to the king and the princess, and he was obliged to borrow money from his coachman to give something to the servants. He drove to Dublin, sold his coach and horses, and paid his servants, and then hadn't one shilling to rub again another in his pocket. He then exchanged his clothes for common things and some little money to boot, and set out on foot towards home. He was eating his piece of bread and his bit of cold bacon next day, when who should come up to him but the very same beggarwoman. Well, they bade one another the time of day, and he shared his meal with her. The same night he had the same vision, but the lady checked him for showing his magic purse to any one, and told him she'd try him once more with another gift. She laid a cloak on the bed, and said that while he kept it on he could be any where he wished. When his eyes opened next morning he saw the cloak, sure enough, and then he began to recollect what a long time the king was fiddling with his purse. "As sure as fate," said he, "*he* has it: what a deceitful old rogue! I'll soon see whether he's guilty or not." He put on the cloak, and wished himself in the king's bed-room. And there he was while you'd wink your eye, and there was the king with a miserly face on him, reckoning piles of guineas, an old night-cap on his head, and a week's growth of beard about his mouth. The purse was on the table, and his trembling fingers pulling out guinea after guinea. "Ah, you wicked old man," says Gilla, "is this the way you treated me?" He darted on the purse, but the king's fingers were like a vice, and he roared out, "Thieves, thieves! murder, robbery!" In run three or four servants, and on Gilla they pounced. He had nothing for it but to run to the window, throw it up, and dart out. *Ovoch!* his cloak caught in the sash, and he was glad to light on the ground with sound bones. To the heels with him, and as it was early, and few stirring, he got away.

So he was on the *shuchraan* [helpless condition] again, and set out for home with a few shillings he had still left. To make a long story short, he met the beggarwoman again, had a vision again, and this time he got a bugle-horn that would make all the soldiers that ever heard it, follow him and fight for him.

So he turned back, and never stopped till he came to where the king was standing at his window reviewing his troops. As soon as Gilla came up, he blew his bugle, and all the soldiers shouted out, and gathered round him, and asked him what they'd do for him.

"I'll soon show you that," said he. So he stepped over to where the king was standing very much surprised, and said; "No one could treat another worse than you did me; but if you give me the princess in marriage, and allow me back my purse and my cloak, I'll make peace and alliance with you." "I must first consult my ministers," said the king, "but you'll have my answer before nine o'clock to-morrow." So Gilla camped his men in the lawn, and he had a nice tent to himself that night.

At dawn he was awoke by some one fumbling about in the tent, and what did he see but the treacherous king with his own magic cloak upon him, taking down the bugle-horn where he negligently left it the evening before, instead of keeping it about his own neck. "Oh, you old robber!" said he, springing out at him, but the horn was in his hands, the cloak on his back, and himself away like a *sighe gaoithe* [fairy blast]. Gilla knew he had no time to lose. He popped on his breeches and coat, and was soon making his ground good. It was time, for he was hardly clear of the sleeping soldiers when the bugle was heard sounding at the king's window, and the soldiers all dressing themselves in the greatest hurry to run and hear his commands.

He was worse off now than ever. He sat down in a dry ditch to eat his bread and bacon in the afternoon, but his beggar woman never came near him, and at night he had no shelter but a couple of trees. He made his bed on dry grass under one of them, and he had a vision of the same beautiful lady; but this time she had displeasure on her face. He thought she was going to speak once or twice, but she stopped herself just as her lips were opening. When he woke, it was a fine sunny morning, and he found himself hungry. Over his head were the loveliest coloured apples, and in the other tree some dull-coloured pears. Up he stretched his hand, and plucked an apple, and ate it. It was very sweet, but before he could get another into his mouth he felt something queer about his nose. It was tickling him, and beginning to feel very heavy, and before you could count three, the end of it was down on the ground, and ploughing away through the grass. "Oh, Gracious!" says he, "what's this for?" But while he spoke, he felt it pulling his head down, so that he was obliged to squat as low as he could to ease his face of the weight. The end of his nose was now at the very end of the field.

I cant't tell, nor could you feel, the state he was in, for, please God, nothing of the kind will ever happen to one of ourselves; but when he was looking at it running over the ditch of the field, a pear dropped at his feet out of the next tree. "Who knows," said he, "but this is a God-send?" So he got a bit of it into his mouth as well as his nose would let him, and the first swallow he made, off went the new nose, and the near end kept creeping and curling away, ding-dong, after the far end.

"Oh, thanks be to Goodness," said he, "and thank you heartily, my good fairy! I think my wicked old father-in-law (that is to be) won't escape me this time."

He had some trifle of money left, and with this he bought an old woman's cloak and bonnet, and a little basket, and plucked off some apples and pears, and away with him to the town outside the palace.

That day after dinner, the butler handed the king three lovely apples, that he said the fruit-seller in the town brought up an hour before. The king could hardly persuade himself to taste any of them, they looked so nice. At last he put a piece of one in his mouth, but it was hardly in his stomach when his nose was down on the carpet, over to the wall, up on the window stool, out over the frame, down the wall, and into the garden. Oh, such a fright! such cries, and such screeches as came out of the mouths of every one in the room; and still the nose went on through the garden and out on the lawn. The king could not stir out of his seat on the carpet, but, as well as he could, he bade a dozen of doctors be sent for. They came, but they could do nothing, and messengers were coming and going every minute to see and bring back word how far the end was getting. It wasn't growing so fast since it got beyond the lawn, but still it was getting on, and the doctors ordered sentries to be stationed all along for fear of a horse treading on it, or a cart wheel running over it.

No one went asleep in the palace that night but the scullery maid and nine of the doctors. The king thought morning would never come, and when he inquired at last where the end of his nose was, he was told it was near the river that lay between his dominions and the next king's, but only going an inch in a minute.

About sunrise, some one came in to tell that a poor-looking man was asking leave to come in to try to cure the king. So he was let in, but told that his head would go off if he done any harm. "Oh, if his Majesty is in a good state of mind, I'll cure him in spite of the divel himself." He gave him a small bit of a pear which he took out of a basket, and it was no sooner down than the nose grew an inch less in the round, the king was able to raise his head a little, and the far off sentries shouted that the nose was gone back half a mile.

"Now, my liege," says the man, "if your conscience is good, I will bring it within its own bounds the next offer. Have you any restitution to make to anybody?" "N-n-n-no!" says he. Then he gave him a bit of fruit, and the king let a roar. His nose was now thicker than it ever was, and the sentries cried to those next them, and these to the others, and those to the sentries in the garden, that the enlarged end was now just at the very bank of the river.

"No use in blindfolding the divel in the dark," says the man. "You'll be lost horse and foot if you don't confess and restore the goods." "Well, I own that I took the bugle of the Gilla na Gruaga Donna from him. Bring that horn from my bed's head, some of you, and give it to the doctor." It was done, another bit of fruit given, and a great shout was heard, "A mile off o' the nose." "Your Majesty has not confessed all. Your nose might as well be seven miles longer for any comfort or rest it will give you." "Well, I have the magic cloak of the same man." The cloak was brought and the man buttoned it round his neck; another bit, and the end of the nose was in the middle of the lawn.

"Which will your Majesty make full restitution or stay as you are?" "I don't care: I'll keep the purse if the end of my nose was at Halifax." But away began the nose to plough again, and more and more the tickling feeling went on. "Here," says he at last, "is the only thing left," and he pulled the purse out of his pocket. "*Sarra* do him good with it!" He threw it to the man, and the remainder of the pear was given him. Down dropped the additional handle from the right nose, and went curling and crackling out of the room, out of the garden, and out of the lawn. "Seize on that rascal!" said the king; but Gilla, for it was he, blew a blast on his bugle, and every one in the room was rushing to tear the daylights out of the king, their master. He held out against the match as long as he could, but the people were all going to dethrone him. So he consented, and if the youth of the brown hair and his princess were not a good and happy couple, I wonder where are such to be found.

SHAN AN OMADHAN AND HIS MASTER.

A POOR woman had three sons. The eldest and second eldest were cunning clever fellows, but they called the youngest Shān an Omadhan, because they thought he was no better than a simpleton. The eldest got tired of staying at home, and said he'd go look for service. He staid away a whole year, and then came back one day, dragging one foot after the other, and a poor wizened face on him, and he as cross as two sticks. When he was rested and got something to eat, he told them how he got service with the *Bodach Liath* of *Tuaim an Drochaigh* [Gray Churl of the Townland of Mischance], and that the agreement was, whoever would first say he was sorry for his bargain, should get an inch wide of the skin of his back, from shoulder to hips, taken off. If it was the master, he should also pay double wages; if it was the servant, he should get no wages at all. "But the thief," says he, "gave me so little to eat, and kept me so hard at work, that flesh and blood couldn't stand it; and when he asked me once, when I was in a passion, if I was sorry for my bargain, I was mad enough to say I was, and here I am disabled for life."

Vexed enough were the poor mother and brothers; and the second eldest said on the spot he'd go and take service with the Gray Churl, and punish him by all the annoyance he'd give him till he'd make him say he was sorry for his agreement. "Oh, won't I be glad to see the skin coming off the old villain's back!" said he. All they could say had no effect: he started off for the Townland of Mischance, and in a twelvemonth he was back just as miserable and helpless as his brother.

All the poor mother could say didn't prevent Shān an Omadhan from starting to see if he was able to regulate the Bodach Liath. He agreed with him for a year for twenty pounds, and the terms were the same.

"Now, Shān," said the Bodach Liath, "if you refuse to do anything you are able to do, you must lose a month's wages." "I'm satisfied," said Shān; "and if you stop me from doing a thing after telling me to do it, you are to give me an additional month's wages." "I am satisfied." says the master. "Or if you blame me for obeying your orders, you must give the same." "I am satisfied," said the master again.

The first day that Shān served he was fed very poorly, and was worked to the saddleskirts. Next day he came in just before the dinner was sent up to the parlour. They were taking the goose off the spit, but well becomes Shān, he whips a knife off the dresser, and cuts off one side of the breast, one leg and thigh, and one wing, and fell to. In came the master, and began to abuse him for his assurance.

"Oh, you know, master, you're to feed me, and wherever the goose goes won't have to be filled again till supper. Are you sorry for our agreement?" The master was going to cry out he was, but he bethought himself in time. "Oh no, not at all," said he. "That's well," said Shān.

Next day Jack was to go clamp turf on the bog. They wern't sorry to have him away from the kitchen at dinner time. He didn't find his breakfast very heavy on his stomach; so he said to the mistress, "I think, ma'am, it will be better for me to get my dinner now, and not lose time coming home from the bog." "That's true, Shān," said she. So she brought out a good cake, and a print of butter, and a bottle of milk, thinking he'd take them away to the bog. But Shān kept his seat, and never drew rein till bread, butter, and milk went down the red lane. "Now, mistress," said he, "I'll be earlier at my work to-morrow if I sleep comfortably on the sheltery side of a clamp [pile of dry peat] on dry grass, and not be coming here and going back. So you may as well give me my supper, and be done with the day's trouble." She gave him that, thinking he'd take it to the bog; but he fell to on the spot, and did not leave a scrap to tell tales on him; and the mistress was a little astonished.

He called to speak to the master in the haggard, and said he, "What are servants asked to do in this country after *aten* their supper?" "Nothing at all, but to go to bed." "Oh, very well, sir." He went up on the stable-loft, stripped, and lay down, and some one that saw him told the master. He came up. "Shān, you anointed *sthronshuch*, what do you mean?" "To go to sleep, master. The mistress, God bless her, is after giving me my breakfast, dinner, and supper, and yourself told me that bed was the next thing. Do you blame me, sir?" "Yes, you rascal, I do." "Hand me out one pound thirteen and fourpence, if you please, sir." "One divel and thirteen imps, you tinker! what for?" "Oh, I see, you've forgot your bargain. Are you sorry for it?" "Oh, ya—NO, I mean. I'll give you the money after your nap."

Next morning early, Jack asked how he'd be employed that day. "You are to be holding the plough in that fallow, outside the paddock." The master went over about nine o'clock to see what kind of a ploughman was Shan, and what did he see but the little boy driving the bastes, and the sock and coulter of the plough skimming along the sod, and Shan pulling ding-dong again' the horses. "What are you doing, you conthrary thief?" said the master. "An' aint I strivin' to hold this divel of a plough, as you told me; but that *ounkrawn* of a boy keeps whipping on the bastes in spite of all I say; will you speak to him?" "No, but I'll speak to you. Didn't you know, you bosthoon, that when I said 'holding the plough,' I meant reddening the ground." "Faith an' if you did, I wish you had said so. Do you blame me for what I have done?" The master caught himself in time, but he was so stomached, he said nothing. "Go on and redden the ground now, you knave, as other ploughmen do." "An' are you sorry for our agreement?" "Oh, not at all, *mauya* [forsooth]!" Shan ploughed away like a good workman all the rest of the day.

In a day or two the master bade him go and mind the cows in a field that had half of it under young corn. "Be sure, particularly," said he, "to keep Browney from the wheat; while she's out of mischief there's no fear of the rest." About noon, he went to see how Shan was doing his duty, and what did he find but Jack asleep with his face to the sod, Browney grazing near a thorn-tree, one end of a long rope round her horns, and the other end round the tree, and the rest of the beasts all trampling and eating the green wheat. Down came the switch on Shan. "Shan, you vagabone, do you see what the cows are at?" "And do you blame me, master?" "To be sure, you lazy, sluggard, I do?" "Hand me out one pound thirteen and fourpence, master. You said if I only kept Browney out of mischief, the rest would do no harm. There she is as harmless as a lamb. Are you sorry for hiring me, master?" "To be—that is, not at all. I'll give you your money when you go to dinner. Now, understand me; don't let a cow go out of the field nor into the wheat the rest of the day." "Never fear, master!" and neither did he. But the bodach would rather than a great deal he had not hired him.

The next day three heifers were missing, and the master bade Jack go in search of them. "Where will I look for them?" said Shan. "Oh, every place likely and unlikely for them all to be in." The bodach was getting very exact in his words. When he was coming into the bawn at dinner-time, what work did he find Jack at but pulling armfulls of the thatch off the roof, and peeping into the holes he was making? "What are you doing there, you rascal?" "Sure, I'm looking for the heifers, poor things!" "What would bring them there?" "I don't think anything could bring them in it; but I looked first into the likely places, that is, the cow-houses, and the pastures, and the fields next 'em, and now I'm looking in the unlikeliest place I can think of. Maybe it's not pleasing to you it is." "And to be sure it isn't pleasing to me, you aggravating *googein* [goosecap]!" "Please sir, hand me one pound thirteen and four pence before you sit down to your dinner. I'm afraid it's sorrow that's on you for hiring me at all." "May the div—oh no; I'm not sorry. Will you begin if you please, and put in the thatch again, just as if you were doing it for your mother's cabin?" "Oh, faith I will, sir, with a heart and a half;" and by the time the farmer came out from his dinner, Shan had the roof better than it was before, for he made the boy give him new straw.

Says the master when he came out, "Go, Shan, and look for the heifers, and bring them home." "And where will I look for 'em?" "Go and search for them as if they were your own." The heifers were all in the paddock before sunset.

Next morning, says the bodach, "Jack, the path across the bog to the pasture is very bad; the sheep does be sinking in it every step; go and make it a good path with the sheep's feet." About an hour after he came to the edge of the bog, and what did he find Shan at but sharpening a carving knife, and the sheep standing or grazing round. "Is this the way you are mending the path, Shan?" said he. "Everything must have a beginning, master," said Shan, "and a thing well begun is half done. I am sharpening the knife, and I'll have the feet off every sheep in the flock while you'd be blessing yourself." "Feet off my sheep, you anointed rogue! and what would you be taking their feet off for?" "An' sure to mend the path as you told me. Says you, 'Shan, *dean staidhear*, &c., make a path with the feet of the sheep.'" "Oh, you fool, I meant make good the path for the sheep's feet." "It's a pity you did'nt say so, master. Hand me out one pound thirteen and fourpence if you don't like me to finish my job." "Divel do you good with your one pound thirteen and fourpence!" "It's better pray than curse, master. Maybe you're sorry for your bargain?" "And to be sure I am——not yet, any way."

The next night the bodach was going to a wedding; and says he to Jack, before he set out: "I'll leave at midnight, and I wish you to come and be with me home, for fear I might be overtaken with the drink. If you're there before, you may *throw a sheep's eye* at me, and I'll be sure to see that they'll give you something for yourself."

About eleven o'clock, while the bodach was in great spirits, he felt something clammy hit him on the cheek. It fell beside his tumbler, and what was it but the eye of a sheep, and a very ugly looking article it was. Well, he could'nt imagine who threw it at him, or why it was thrown at him. After a little he got a blow on the other cheek, and still it was by another sheep's eye. Well, he was very vexed, but he thought better to say nothing. In two minutes more, when he was opening his mouth to take a sup, another sheep's eye was slapped into it. He sputtered it out, and cried, "Man o' the house, isn't it a great shame for you to have any one in the room that would do such a nasty thing?" "Master," says Shan, "don't blame the honest man. Sure it's only myself that was throwin' them sheep's eyes at you, to remind you I was here, and that I wanted to drink the bride and bridegroom's health. You know yourself bade me." "I know that you are a great rascal; and where did you get the eyes?" "An' where would I get 'em but in the heads of your own sheep? Would you have me meddle with the bastes of any neighbour, who might put me in the *Stone Jug* [gaol] for it?" "*Mo chuma* [my sorrow] that ever I had the bad luck to meet with you."

" You're all witness," said Jack, "that my master says he is sorry for having met with me. My time is up. Master, hand me over double wages, and come into the next room, and lay yourself out like a man that has some decency in him, till I take a strip of skin an inch broad from your shoulder to your hip." Every one shouted out against that; but, says Shan, " You didn't hinder him when he took the same strips from the backs of my two brothers, and sent them home in that state, and penniless, to their poor mother." When the company heard the rights of the business, they were only too eager to see the job done. The bodach bawled and roared, but there was no help at hand. He was stripped to his hips, and laid on the floor in the next room, and Jack had the carving knife in his hand ready to begin. "Now, you cruel old villian," said he, giving the knife a couple of scrapes along the floor, "I'll make you an offer. Give me, along with my double wages, two hundred pounds to support my poor brothers, and I'll do without the strap." "No!" said he, "I'd let you skin me from head to foot first." "Here goes then," said Shan with a grin, but the first little scar he gave, bodach roared out, " Stop your hand; I'll give the money."

"Now, neighbours," said Shān, "you mustn't think worse of me than I deserve. I wouldn't have the heart to take an eye out of a rat itself; I got half a dozen of them from the butcher, and only used three of them."

So all came again into the other room, and Shan was made sit down, and everybody drank his health, and he drank everybody's health at one offer. And six stout fellows saw himself and the bodach home, and waited in the parlour while he went up and brought down the two hundred guineas, and double wages for Shan himself. When he got home, he brought the summer along with him to the poor mother and the disabled brothers; and he was no more *Shan an Omadhan* in the people's mouths, but *Shan a' Ruisgeach*, "Jack the Skinner."

THE PRINCESS IN THE CAT-SKINS.

THERE was once a queen that was left a widow with one daughter, who was as good and handsome as any girl could be. But her mother wasn't satisfied to remain without a husband; so she married again, and a very bad choice she made. Her second husband treated her very badly; and she died soon after. Well, would you ever think of the widower taking it into his head to marry the young princess at the end of a year? She was as shocked as she could be when he made her the offer, and burst out a crying. "I took you too sudden," said he. "Sleep on it, and you can give me an answer to-morrow."

She was in great trouble all the rest of the day, and when the evening came she went out into the paddock, where a beautiful filly she used to ride was grazing. "Oh my poor beast!" said she, "I'm sure if you knew my trouble you'd pity me." "I do know your trouble, and I pity you, and I'll help you too," says the filly. "I'm the fairy that watched over you from the time you were born, and I am here near you since your mother married the second time. Your stepfather is an enchanter, but he'll find me too strong for him. Don't seem shocked when he'll ask your consent to-morrow, but say you must have first a dress of silk and silver thread that will fit into a walnut shell. He'll promise, and will be able to get it made too, but I'll bother his spinner and his weaver long enough before he'll get it wove, and his seamstress after that, before it's sewed."

The princess *done* as she was bid, and the enchanter was in great joy; but he was kept in great trouble and anger for a full half year before the dress was ready to go on the princess. At last it was fitted, and he asked her was she ready to be his wife. "I'll tell you to-morrow," said she. So she went to consult her filly in the paddock.

Well, the next day he put the question to her again, and she said that she couldn't think of marrying any one till she had another dress of silk and gold thread that would fit in a walnut shell. "I wish you had mentioned itself and the silver dress together. Both could have been done at the same time. No matter: I'll get it done." What-

6

ever trouble the spinner and the weaver and the seamstress had with the other dress, they had twice it with this; but at last it was tried on, and fitted like a glove.

"Well now," says *Fear Dhorrach*, "I hope your'e satisfied, and won't put off the wedding again." "Oh, you must forgive me," said she, "for my vanity." She was talking to the filly the evening before. "I can't do without a dress of silk thread as thick as it can be with diamonds and pearls no larger than the head of a minnikin pin. Three is a lucky number, you know." "Well, I wish you had mentioned this at first, and the three could be making together. Now this is the very last thing you'll ask, I expect." "Oh, I'll never ask another, you may depend, till I'm married." She didn't say till *we're* married. The dress came home at last. Well, the same evening she found on her bed another made from bottom to top of cat-skins, and this she put on. She put her three walnut-shells in her pocket, and then stole out to the stable, where she found her filly with a bridle in her mouth, and the nicest side-saddle ever you saw on her back. Away they went, and when the light first appeared in the sky they were a hundred miles away.

They stopped at the edge of a wood, and the princess was very glad to rest herself on a bunch of dry grass at the foot of a tree. She wasn't a minute there when she fell asleep; and soundly she did sleep, till she was woke up by the blowing of bugles and the yelping of beagles. She jumped up in a fright. There was no filly near her, but half a hundred spotted hounds were within forty perches of her, yelling out of them like vengeance. I needn't tell you she was frightened. She had hardly power to put one foot past the other, and she'd be soon tore into giblets by the dogs on account of her dress, but a fine young hunter leaped over their heads, and they all fell back when he shook his whip and shouted at them. So he came to the princess, and there she was as wild-looking as you please, with her cat-skins hanging round her, and her face and hands and arms as brown as a berry, from a wash she put on herself before she left home. Well that didn't hinder her features from being handsome, and the prince was astonished at her beauty and her colour and her dress, when he found she was a stranger, and alone in the world. He got off his horse, and walked side by side with her to his palace, for he was the young king of that country.

He sent for his housekeeper when he came to the hall-door, and bid her employ the young girl about whatever she was fit for, and then set off to follow the hounds again. Well, there was great tittering in the servants' hall among the maids at her colour and her dress, and the ganders of footmen would like to be joking with her, but she made no freedom with one or the other, and when the butler thought to give her a kiss, she gave him a light slap on the jaw that wouldn't kill a fly, but he felt as if a toothache was at him for eight and forty-hours. By my word, the other buckeens did not give her an excuse to raise her hand to them. Well, she was so silent and kept herself to herself so much, that she was no favourite, and they gave her nothing better to do than help the scullery maid, and at night she had to put up with a little box of a place under the stairs for a bed-room.

The next day, when the prince returned from hunting, he sent word to the housekeeper by the whipper-in to let the new servant bring him up a basin and towel till he'd wash before dinner. "Oh, ho!" says the cook, "there's an honour for Cat-skin. I'm here for forty years and never was asked to do such a thing; how grand we are! *purshuin* to all impedent people!" The princess didn't mind their jibes and their jeers. She took up the things, and the prince delayed her ever so long with remarks and questions, striving to get out of her what rank of life she was born in. As little as she said he guessed her to be a lady. I suppose it is as hard for a lady or gentleman to pass for a vulgarian, as for one of us to act like one of the quality. Well to be sure! all the cold and scornful noses that were in the big kitchen before her; and it was, "Cat-skin, will you hand me this? Cat-skin, will you grease my shoes? Cat-skin, will you draw a jug of beer for me?" And she done everything she was asked without a word or a sour look.

Next night the prince was at a ball about three miles away, and the princess got leave from the housekeeper to go early to bed. Well, she couldn't get herself to lie down:

she was in a fever like; she threw off her outside dress, and she stepped out into the lawn to get a little fresh air. There what did she behold but her dear filly under a tree. She ran over, and threw her arms round her neck, and kissed her face, and began to cry. "No time for crying!" says the filly. "Take out the first walnut shell you got." She did so, and opened it. "Hold what's inside over your head," said the other, and in a moment the silk and silver dress wrapped her round as if a dozen *manty-makers* were after spending an hour about it. "Get on that stump," says the filly, "and jump into the side-saddle." She did so, and in a few minutes they were at the hall door of the castle where the ball was. There she sprung from her saddle, and walked into the hall. Lights were in the hall and everywhere, and nothing could equal the glitter of the princess's robes and the accoutrements of her steed. It was like the curling of a stream in the sun.

You may believe that the quality were taken by surprise, when the princess walked in among them as if they were the lords and ladies in her father's court. The young king came forward as he saw the rest were a little cowed, and bade her good evening and welcome; and they talked whatever way kings and queens and princesses do, and he made her sit on his own seat of honour, and took a stool or a chair near her, and if he wasn't delighted and surprised, her features were so like the scullery maid's, leave it till again.

They had a fine supper and a dance, and the prince and she danced, and every minute his love for her was increasing, but at last she said she should go. Every one was sorry, and the prince more than anyone, and he came with her to the hall, and asked might he see her safe home. But she showed him her filly and excused herself. Said he, "I'll have my brown horse brought, and myself and my servants will attend you." "Hand me up on my filly," says she, "first of all," and, be the laws, I don't know how princes put princesses on horseback. Maybe one of the servants stoops his back, and the prince goes on one knee, and she steps first on his knee and then on the servant's back, and then sits in the saddle. Anyhow she was safe up, and she took the prince's hand, and bid him good night, and the filly and herself were away like a flash of lightning in the dark night.

Well, everything appeared dismal enough when he went back to where a hundred tongues were going hard and fast about the lady in the dazzling dress.

Next morning he bid his footman ask the girl in the cat-skin to bring him hot water and a towel for him to shave. She came in as modest and backward as you please; but whenever the prince got a peep at her face, there were the beautiful eyes and nose and mouth of the lady in the glittering dress, but all as brown as a bit of bogwood. He thought to get a little talk out of her, but dickens a word would come out of her mouth but *yes* or *no*. And when he asked her was she of high birth, she turned off the discourse and would'nt say one thing or the other; and when he asked would she like to put on nice clothes and be about his mother, she refused just as if he asked her to drown herself. So he found he could make nothing of her, and let her go down stairs.

There was another great ball in a week's time, and the very same thing took place again. There was the princess, and the dress she had on was of silk and gold thread, and the darlintest little gold crown in the world over her purty curling hair. If the prince was in love before, he was up to his eyes in it this time; but while they were going on with the nicest sweet talk, says she, "I'm afraid, prince, that you are in the habit of talking lovingly to every girl you meet." Well, he was very eager to prove he was not. "Then," said she, "a little bird belied you as I was coming through the wood. He said that you weren't above talking soft even to a young servant girl with her skin as brown as a berry, and her dress no better than cat-skin." "I declare to you, princess," said he, "there is such a girl at home; and if her skin was as white as yours, and her dress the same, no eye could see a bit of differ between you." "Oh, thankee, prince!" says she, "for the compliment; it's time for me to be going." Well, he thought to mollify her, but she curled her upper lip and cocked her nose, and wasn't long till she left, the way she did before. While she was getting on her filly, he almost went down on his knees to her to make it up. So at last she smiled, and said, "If I can make up my mind to forgive you, I'll come to the next ball without invitation." So she was away, and when they came under the tree in the lawn she took the upper hem of her dress in her fingers and it came off like a glove, and she made her way in at the back door, and into her crib at the stair-foot.

The prince slept little that night, and in the morning he sent his footman to ask the girl in the cat-skins to bring up a needle and thread to sew a button on his shirt-sleeve. He watched her fingers, and saw they were small and of a lovely shape; and when one of them touched his wrist, it felt as soft and delicate as silk. All he could say got nothing out of her only, "It wasn't a nice thing for a prince to speak in that way to a girl of low degree, and he boasting of it after to princesses and great ladies." Well, how he did begin to deny anything so ungenteel, but the button was sewed, and she skipped away down stairs.

The third night came, and she shook the dress of silk and pearls and diamonds over her, and the nicest crown of the same on her head. As grand and beautiful as she was before, she was twice as grand now; and the lords and ladies hardly dared to speak above their breaths, and the prince thought he was in heaven. He asked her at last would she be his queen, and not keep him in misery any longer, and she said she would, if she was sure he wouldn't ask Miss Cat-skin the same question next day. Oh, how he spoke, and how he promised! He asked leave to see her safe home, but she wouldn't agree. "But don't be downcast," said she, "you will see me again sooner than you think; and if you know me when you meet me next, we'll part no more." Just as she was sitting in her saddle, and the prince was holding her hand, he slipped a dawny limber ring of gold on one finger. It was so small and so nice to the touch he thought she wouldn't feel it. "And now, my princess," says he to himself, "I think I'll know you when I meet you."

Next morning he sent again for the scullery girl, and she came and made a *curtchy*. "What does your majesty want me to do?" said she. "Only to advise me which of these two suits of clothes would look best on me; I'm going to be married." "Ah, how could the likes of me be able to advise you? Is the rich dressed lady, that I heard the footmen talking about, to be your queen?" "Yourself is as likely to be my wife as that young lady." "Then who is it?" "Yourself, I tell you." "Myself! How can your majesty joke that way on a poor girl? They say you're promised to the lady of the three rich dresses." "I'm promised to no one but yourself. I asked you twice already to be my queen; I ask you now the third time." "Yes, and maybe after all, you'll marry the lady of the dresses." "You promised you'd have me if I knew you the next time we'd meet. This is the next time. If I don't know you, I know my ring on your fourth finger." She looked, and there it was sure enough. Maybe she didn't blush. "Will your majesty step into the next room for a minute," said she, "and leave me by myself?" He did so, and when she opened the door for him again, there she was with the brown stain off her face and hands, and her dazzling dress of silk and jewels on her. Wasn't he the happy prince, and she the happy princess? And weren't the noisy servants *lewd* of themselves when they saw poor Cat-skin in her royal dress saying the words before the priest? They didn't put off their marriage, and there was the fairy now in the appearance of a beautiful woman; and if I was to tell you about the happy life they led, I'd only be tiring you.

———>◆◆◆<———

THE WELL AT THE WORLD'S END.

ONCE there was a king that had three sons, and he was so sick that no one thought he'd ever recover. They went to consult a wise old hermit that lived in a wood near, and he said that nothing would cure the king but a draught from the World's-End water. So the eldest son thought to himself, —"I'll set out to bring this drink, and then I'll be sure to get all the kingdom from my father when he's about to die." So he got leave from his father and set out. He went first to the hermit, and asked him whereabouts was the "End of the world," and the hermit gave him directions how he'd go to it. He was to cross seven seas, and seven lakes, and seven rivers, and seven mountains, and seven hills, and seven commons, and then he'd see before him a castle of brass, and all he knew farther was that the Well of the World's-End water was in the garden of that castle.

So the prince set out, and one day he sat down by the way side to eat some bread and cold meat. Up came a poor, ragged, withered old woman, and asked him to give her a bit to keep the life in her. "Go away, you old hag, out of that!" said he, "I have nothing for you." "Well, well," said she; "God help the poor! But would your majesty tell a poor body where you're going?" "What's that to you, you old witch?" said he again; "go about your business, and don't be bothering me!" "Well, prince," said she, "your birth is better than your manners anyhow. Still, for sake of the king and queen that owns you, I'll give you an advice. Never blow your bugle till you first draw your sword, and when you're on duty resist temptation." "Thank you for nothing," said he. "I've got enough of you." So she went away, muttering.

Well, when he passed the remaining hills and commons and lakes and rivers, he saw far off the castle of brass, and in good time he arrived at it. There was a bugle horn hanging by the door, and, without minding the old woman's advice, he put it to his mouth and blew it without thinking of his sword. Open flew the door, and out on him rushed two lions roaring like thunder. He thought to pull out his sword, but they kept on biting and scratching and tearing him till he thought he was done for. "Go then," says one of them. "You are a bad prince, but you are on a good business, and we'll give you your life." Well, he stumbled in, and there he was in a long hall, and at each side were standing fifty knights in armour, holding up their spears, and all dead asleep. His heart beat, but he passed on, and in the next hall there was a beautiful princess with a crown on her head, and she sitting on a throne. He approached her, and made all sorts of nice speeches to her, but she reminded him of the business he was on, and told him there was no time to be lost. "After passing through the next hall," said she, "you will be in the garden where the well of the World's-End water springs. If you are not out of the castle with your bottle full before the clock strikes twelve, there's a heavy doom hanging over you."

In the next hall there was a table laid out with the finest food and drink the prince ever saw, and he was so tired with walking, and so spent in his struggle with the lions, that he fell to. The clock still wanted a quarter; he'd have time enough. When it was two minutes before the hour he went into the garden, and he was so hot, and it was so delightful in the shade, for the well was under a tree, that he sat down on a garden seat, and felt that it would be as much as his life was worth to be obliged to leave it. While he was half dozing, the clock began to strike. Oh, murder! he began to fill the bottle as fast as he could, but it was on the seventh stroke before he had it filled. Seven, eight, nine, ten,—he was in the dining room, and in the lady's room. It was eleven when he was running into the knight's hall, but he was only in the middle of it when bang went twelve, and the knights struck the ends of their spears on the ground, and came round him in a ring. What could his single sword do against so many. He hadn't even power to draw it. A rough fellow with a bush of red hair on his head came in, and tied him hand and foot, and threw him into a dungeon.

Well, his place was empty at home for half a year, and then his next brother set out; and to make a long story short, he behaved the same way and got the same treatment. Last of all the youngest set off, and very differently he behaved to the poor old woman, and she gave him when they were parting two cakes, and told him what to do with them.

When he reached the castle he drew the sword, and then blew the bugle horn. Open flew the doors, and out rushed the lions. But he held out a cake to each beast, and down they sat like two lambs to eat them. He went through the first hall, and went on one knee before the lady in the second. There was pleasure on her face at the sight of him, but she told him there was no delay to be made. So he passed through the next room without taking bit or sup, though he felt as hungry and thirsty as he could be. The greatest temptation was on him when he went into the garden—he was so hot and faint—to sit on the seat and enjoy the cool, but he didn't give way. He filled his bottle and returned through the dining hall without sitting down to refresh himself. He would have stopped to speak to the lady, but she warned him away, and he had no temptation to stop between the two rows of the men in the iron armour. He passed the lions who were still eating their cakes, and when he closed the door after him he blew the bugle with all his force. The sound came out like thunder where the rocks are on every side, and before it ceased, down came the castle as if the sky was falling. The stones never sunk into the earth, they vanished after seeming to fall a little, though the noise they made was frightful. When all was cleared, there was neither lions, nor armed men, nor loaded tables to be seen. The princess was sitting on a grassy ridge, and the two brothers lying unbound in a furrow.

There was great joy among the four, for the princess was released from enchantment as well as the brothers from their chains. They set out for the palace, but they were met on the road by a coach and horses, which the princess said were sent by a powerful friend she had. The elder brothers saw that either of them had little chance to be her husband: so at times they plotted together, and when they were near home, at the very spot where the old woman met with them all, they fell on their youngest brother, tied him neck and heels, and left him inside of the wood to die of pain and hunger. The princess gave one cry when she saw her prince seized, but never opened her mouth after till they reached the palace. The brothers then made her swear that she would never reveal who got the water, or what became of the youngest prince, and she did so without the smallest objection.

Well, there was great joy in the palace when the princes and the beautiful lady arrived, and when they told that they returned with the water. They said they knew nothing of their youngest brother, and that made the king sad. However, the eldest son called for a cup of gold, and poured in some of the water, and handed it to his father. He drank some of it, but laid down the cup in a moment. He said he was seized with a colic, and cried out with the pain. "Let me give the drink," said the second eldest, "you know it was I that got it." He took up the cup and handed it to the king; but as bad as he was before, he was twice worse now; and how the brothers looked at one another! They begged the princess to hand the cup next, but she didn't seem to hear them. Well, all were at their wits' end, when in walked a tall beggarwoman and her son, and both in rags. "Will your majesty allow this young man to hand you the cup?" "Oh, if it is of any use, let him do so; but if not, he'll be torn between wild horses." "Oh, very well." The young man went forward, and presented the cup, but the king turned all manner of colours, and twisted his face into a dozen of forms before he'd let it to his lips again. The moment he swallowed one sup his late pains left him, and his old sickness was gone, and he stood up in perfect health. He was about opening his mouth to thank the boy and his mother, but she touched him with a rod she had in her hands, and his rags were gone, and there was the youngest prince in his own dress, and as handsome as the May!

A fine looking woman was where the beggar stood a minute since, and she wasn't long about explaining the whole wickedness of the brothers. They looked for all the world like two dogs that had lost their tails, and seemed to wish to sink into the ground. They were banished the same day from the court, and the next day came on the marriage of the youngest son with the enchanted lady.

———>◆◆◆<———

THE POOR GIRL THAT BECAME A QUEEN.

A COTTIER-MAN and his daughter lived near a king's palace, and they were so poor that the girl advised her father one day to go to the king, and ask him for three or four acres of land, so that they could keep body and soul together. "Come along with me," said he, "and I will." So when the king was going out to have a walk after his breakfast, they put themselves in his way, and the father made the request. The king granted it: I believe he was pleased with the smoothness of the young girl's face, and the sense he saw in it.

Well, they worked away on the little farm as happy as you please, till one day, when they dug up a golden mortar from under the sod (them is things used by pottecaries to grind their drugs in). "Oh, my!" says the father, "this is the king's property; I'll take it to him; he well deserves it." "Don't, father," says the girl, "he'll ask for the crushing stick along with it." "Crushing stick indeed! he'll be too glad of the bowl." So he wouldn't be persuaded, and be this and be that he was soon sorry enough for it. The king, instead of thanking him for the mortar, asked for the pounder, and when it wasn't to the fore, "Take that man," says he to his guards, "and put him in prison, and keep him on bread and water till he finds the pounding stick."

Well, two days after, the jailer came into the king's presence, and says he, "Maybe your majesty would order the new *presner* to some other place, for he lets no one rest or sleep that's near him, crying out, "Oh, if I'd been said and led by my daughter! Oh, if I'd been said and led by my daughter!" "Send him in to me," says the king. Well, when he came, says the king "What are you *moithering* every one about you for, with your daughter and her advice?" "An' sure, your majesty, if I'd taken it I wouldn't be now in preson. Says I, when I dug up the gold mortar, 'I'll take this to the king, God bless him!' 'Don't, father,' says she, 'he'll be wanten the poundher.'" "Go home," says the king, "and send her to the palace."

Well, she made herself as dasent as she could, and presented herself, and the king was greatly pleased with her comely face and her good sense, and after conversing with her for some time, says he, "I'll give you a riddle. Come here to-morrow neither with your clothes nor without them, neither riding in car nor coach, nor on a beast's back, nor carried in any way, nor walking on your feet. If you do this, I'll tell you more of my mind."

Well, the next day the king was sitting on his door-step, and his lords were standing on each side waiting to see if the girl would find out the riddle, and by my word they were soon at their ease. They heard a clatter outside the bawn, and some one crying out *hub!* and *hoe!* and in came an ass very ill at his ease, for there was a fisherman's net tied to his tail, and the same net was wrapt round my brave girl, who had nothing on her above her waist, and she was neither carried, nor riding, nor walking, but standing on her two big toes in the net, and guiding and whipping the poor *assol*, that was dragging her along very much against his will.

"My brave wise girl that you were!" says the king. "If you won't be my queen I'll have no other;" and married they were off-hand, and lived seven years together in the greatest comfort.

One day some countrymen came to the palace with loads of firewood. One man had a horse, and a mare, and a foal, and another had two bullocks. The foal was gambolling about, and got in between the bullocks, and when they were leaving, the owner of the beasts would not let the little fellow go back to his mother and father; he said the bullocks owned him. The other man complained to the king, but whether he was thinking of something else, or wished to put a greater punishment on the rogue of a bullock-owner next day, he ordered that the foal should be left where he was.

Well, the poor man was *stomached* enough you may depend, and didn't know what to do till he bethought of the queen and her great wit, and her being a cottier-man's daughter. So he asked to see her, and this is the way he acted according to her advice.

Next day the king was passing out on some business, and what should he see in the middle of the road but the owner of the foal hard and fast at work, casting a net in the dust, drawing it in, opening it out, lifting his handfuls of nothing out of it, and pitching them into his sack. "What nonsense is this you're at?" says the king. "You'll take no fish on the yellow high road." "I will, your Majesty, as many as you'll find foals between a pair of bullocks."

"Who told you to say and do this?" said the king. "My own brain," said the man. "I'll let you see the *conthra'ry*," said the king. Put this fellow in prison, and let him neither eat, drink, nor sleep till he confesses who was his adviser."

Well, the poor man held out for three days, till at last he didn't know whether he was dead or alive, and then it came out that he was speaking to the Queen, and when the king was told of it, he sent for her, and this is what he said:— "I ought to've known that an ignorant country girl could never demean herself in a high station. You have let yourself down so low by your *coshering* and *cuggering* with that woodman, that you must go back to your father." Well, she cried and sobbed, but said he, "It's no use, we must part. However, you were a good wife, and you may take with you whatever treasures are in the palace that you value most." "I must submit," says she, "but let us take one meal together, and drink one parting drink before you send me away." "With all my heart," says he. They ate and they drank, and the king didn't rightly remember how she parted from him. Twenty-four hours after, he opened his eyes, and saw nothing round him but the poor walls and furniture of a cabin.

Loudly he called for his servants, but there was no answer, and very surprised and frightened he was. He called louder, and in came his wife—more beautiful than ever she appeared—and threw her arms round his neck. "Oh, have I you still, my darling!" said he; "but where are we?" "In the cabin I was born in," said she. "You gave me leave to bring away what I valued most. I put a sleepy posset in your wine, and got you nicely covered up in a quilt, and carried here."

"Ah, what a headstrong fool I was," said he. "But I hope I'll live long enough to make you forget that one act." I'll let you all fancy how rejoiced the people in the palace were when they saw their king and queen coming back arm and arm. If ourselves lived under such a man and woman, it isn't aten dry potatoes we'd be, one and twenty times a week for novelty.

THE GRATEFUL BEASTS.

THERE was once a young man, and it happened that he had a guinea in his pocket, and was going to some fair or *pattern* or another, and while he was on the way, he saw some little boys scourging a poor mouse they were after catching. "Come, gorsoons," says he, "don't be at that cruel work; here's sixpence for you to buy gingerbread and let him go." They only wanted the wind of the word, and off jumped the mouse. He didn't go much farther, when he overtook another parcel of young *geochachs*, and they tormenting the life out of a poor weasel. Well, he bought him off for a shilling, and went on. The third creature he rescued from a crowd of grown up young rascals was an ass, and he had to give a whole half crown to get him off.

"Now," says poor Neddy, "you may as well take me with you. I'll be of some use carrying you when you're tired." "With all my heart," says Jack. The day was very hot, and the boy sat under a tree to enjoy the cool. As sure as he did he fell asleep without intending it, but he was soon woke up by a wicked looking *bodach* and his two servants. "How dare you let your ass go trespass on my inch" [river meadow] says he, "and do such mischief." "I had no notion he'd do anything of the kind: I dropped asleep by accidence." "Oh be this an' be that! I'll accidence you. Bring out that chest," says he to one of his gillas; and while you'd be sayin' *thrapsticks* they had the poor boy lyin' on the broad of his back in it, and a strong hempen rope tied round it, and himself an' itself flung into the river.

Well, they went away to their business, and poor Neddy stayed roarin' an' bawlin' on the bank, till who should come up but the weasel and the mouse, and they axed him what ailed him. "An' isn't the kind boy that rescued me from them *scoggins* that were tormenting me just now, fastened up in a chest and dhrivin down that terrible river?" "Oh, says the weasel, "he must be the same boy that rescued the mouse and myself. Had he a brown piece on the elbow of his coat?" "The very same." "Come then," says the weasel, "and let us overtake him, and get him out." "By all means," says the others. So the weasel got on the ass's back, and the mouse in his ear, and away with them. They hadn't the trouble of going far, when they see the chest which was stopped among the rushes at the edge of a little island. Over they went, and the weasel and the mouse gnawed the rope till they had the *led* off, and their master out on the bank. Well, they were all very glad, and were conversing together, when what should the weasel spy but a beautiful egg with the loveliest colours on the shell lying down in the shallow water? He wasn't long till he had it up, and Jack was turning it round and round, and admiring it. "Oh, musha, my good friends," says he, "I wish it was in my power to show my gratitude to you, and that I had a fine castle and estate where we could live with full and plenty!" The words were hardly out of his mouth when the beasts and himself found themselves standing on the steps of a castle, and the finest lawn before it that ever you saw.

There was no one inside nor outside to dispute possession with them, and there they lived as happy as kings. They found money enough inside in a cupboard, and the house had the finest furniture in every room, and it was an easy matter to hire servants and labourers.

Jack was standing at his gate one day, as three merchants were passing by with their goods packed on the backs of horses and mules. "Death alive!" says they, what's this for? There was neither castle, nor lawn, nor *three* here the last time we went by."

"True for you!" says Jack. But you shant be the worse for it. Take your beasts into the bawn behind the house, and give 'em a good feed, and if you're not in a hurry, stay and take a bit of dinner with myself." They wished for no better, and after dinner the innocent slob of a Jack let himself be overtaken, and showed them his painted egg, and told 'em every thing that happened him. As sure as the hearth money, one of 'em puts a powder in Jack's next tumbler, and when he woke it was in the island he found himself, with his patched coat on him, and his three friends sitting on their currabingoes near him, and looking very down in the mouth.

"Ah, master!" says the weasel, "you'll never be wise

enough for the thricky people that's in the world. Where did them thieves say they lived, and what's the name that's on 'em ?" Jack scratched his head, and after a little recollected the town. "Come, Neddy," says the weasel, "let us be jogging." So he got on his back, and the mouse in his ear, and the ass *swum* the river, and nothing is said of their travels till they came to the house of the head rogue. The mouse went in, and the ass and the weasel sheltered themselves in a copse outside. He soon came back to them. "Well, what news?" "Dull news enough. He has the egg in a low press in his bed-room, and a pair of cats with fiery eyes watching it night and day, and they chained to the press, and the room door double locked." "Let us go back!" says the ass; we can't do nothing." "Wait," says the weasel."

When sleep time came, says the weasel to the mouse, "Go in at the key hole, and get behind the rogue's head, an' stay two or three hours sucking his hair." "What good in that ?" says the ass. "Wait, an' you'll know," says the weasel. Next morning the merchant was quite mad to find the way his hair was in. "But I'll disappoint you tonight, you thief of a mouse," says he. So he unchained the cats next night, and bid them sit by his bed-side and watch.

Just as he was dropping asleep, the weasel and mouse were outside the door, and gnawing away till they had a hole scooped out at the bottom. In went the mouse, and it was'nt long till he had the egg outside. They were soon on the road again; the mouse in the ass's ear, the weasel on his back, and the egg in the weasel's mouth. When they came to the river, and were swimming across, the ass began to bray. "Hee haw, hee haw!" says he, "is there the likes of me in the world ?" I'm carrying the mouse, and the weasel, and the great enchanted egg, that can do anything. Why don't yous praise me ?" But the mouse was asleep, and the weasel was afraid of opening his mouth. "I'll shake yous off, you ungrateful pack if you don't," says the ass again; and the poor weasel, forgetting himself, cried out, "Oh, don't!" and down went the egg in the deepest pool of the river. "Now you done it," says the weasel, and you may be sure the ass looked very *lewd* of himself. "Oh, what are we to do now, at all, at all?" says he. "Never despair," says the weasel. He looked down into the deep water and cried, "Hear, all you frogs and fish! There is a great army coming to take yous out, and eat yous red raw; look sharp!" "Oh, and what can we do?" says they, coming up to the top. "Gather up all the stones, and hand them to us, and we'll make a big wall on the bank to defend you." They began to work like little divels in a mud wall, and were hard and fast reaching up the pebbles they found on the bottom. At last a big frog came up with the egg in his mouth, and when the weasel had hold of it, he got up in a tree, and cried out, "That will do. The army is frightened and running away." So the poor things were greatly relieved.

You may be sure that Jack was very rejoiced to see his friends and the egg again. They were soon back in their castle and lawn, and when Jack began to feel lonesome he did not find it hard to make out a fine young wife for himself, and his three friends were as happy as the day was long.

THE GILLA RUA.

THE *Gilla Rua* [Red Fellow], when he had no suspicion of you, you might turn him round your little finger, but once he found you were a *cannat*, he'd outwit you if you were as cute as *Cahir-na-Goppal*. He bought a mule one day at the fair, and when he was riding it home, the eldest of three brothers that were neighbours of his, met him, an' axed him what he was after buying. "This brave mule, to be sure," says he. "Mule *inagh!* Oh, my poor Gilla, don't you see it is a thorough-bred ass?" "There's some *shraumogues* on your eyes, my poor man," says Gilla. "Be it so," says the other: "time 'ill tell." A quarter of a mile further he met the second brother. "Good morrow, Gilla." "Good morrow, sir." "Where are you going?" "Home from the fair with this mule I bought." "Mule! Where did you learn to give that name to a common *sturk* of an ass?" "Ah! give us none of your impedence. It is as good a mule as you'd find in Leinster." "We'll see how that's to be; good morning to you."

Off he went, and Gilla began to be troubled. "Can it be that there's anything amiss with my eyes? Here's two honest neighbours that can't have any object in deceiving. If the next man I meet tells me it's an ass, be this and be that I'll make him a present of it." A quarter of a mile further on, who did he meet but the youngest brother? (They laid out the plan early in the fair) "*Morra*, Gilla." "*Morra* kindly," "Where were you?" &c. &c. and the questions and answers went on till the third rogue cursed and swore that the mule was an ass; "And it's an ass that's on his back," says Gilla. "Take him, and be hanged to him!"

Gilla came home, and *Cauth* [Catherine] his housekeeper asked him where was the mule he went to buy. "Tattheration to him for a mule! he turned out to be an ass, and for *sharoose* I bestowed him on so-and-so." "Oh, musha, masther, but you're the sorra's own *gaum*. Sure it was nothing but a thrick laid out between the three unhanged rogues to get your baste from you." Gilla stood for a while in a quanda'ry. "Wait, Cauth," says he, "I'll pay 'em in their own coin."

He went and bought two goats that you wouldn't know one from another. He tied up one in the bawn, with plenty of grass before her, and threw a wallet over the other's back, and led her into town next market day. He was very busy going from the butcher's to the grocer's, and from the grocer's to the mealman's, and putting what he bought into both ends of the wallet. The three rogues saw what he was about, and asked him what it was all for. "It's for a dinner it is, that I'm giving to-day to a few friends, and *yez* three will be heartily welcome along with them. I owe you a kindness for taking that nasty baste off my hands." "Faith an' we'll go with a heart an' a half." "Well, while Jin is carrying the *makins* o' the dinner home, let us wet our whistle." "Why, will the goat go home by herself?" "She will, and give my message to Cauth. Here, Jin; tell Cauth to make the dumplins as she always does, and to boil a couple of heads of our best white cabbage with that bacon, and to put the names of our three neighbours in the pot, &c., &c., &c. There, away with you!" He let the goat loose with her head towards home, cracked his whip, and off went Jin. It's not said that he ever laid eyes on her again. They were just outside the town, and he took the men in to give them share of a half gallon.

Well, they were so eager to see if the goat 'ud do as she was desired, that they did'nt go home to put on their best things, but went straight to Gilla's along with himself when they took their drink.

They saw Jin, as they thought, at her dinner in the bawn, and listened with all their ears cocked while Gilla was questioning Cauth. "Did Jin give you my message?" "Faith an' she did." "What was it she said?" "Ah, sure it was to boil our two best heads of white cabbage, to make the dumplins as I always did, and put our three neighbours' names in with the rest," &c. "What a wonderful animal!" said one brother in a whisper to the others, and they whispered and they *cuggered*. After dinner, says one of them to Gilla; "I'd like to buy that goat of yours. She'd amuse our three wives and the *childher*." They all lived in the same house. "What'll you take for her?" "'Deed I don't wish to part with her, she's a valuable beast, but you're good neighbours, and you never lose what your neigbour gets: you must have her for five an' twenty guineas." "Five and twenty *dhonnasses* (woes)! say ten pounds, and we'll be thinking of it." The end was, that they reckoned twenty guineas into Gilla's hand and took the goat home. May be they did'nt keep their families from getting a wink of sleep that night with all the wonders they told about her.

Next morning says they to their wives, "Have a good fire, and the water at the boil, but don't get anything ready. We'll give you a threat to day. We'll take Jin to town, put the dinner on her back, and send word by her how you're to dress it." "Very well."

When the wallet was filled and the goat sent home with the message, they never minded to see how she behaved, but went in to take share of a quart; but they were home at one o'clock, rather muzzy with the beer they drank. When they came in, they found their wives sitting with their hands across, the table laid out, the spit before the fire, the big pot boiling, but not a sign of food in any quarter. " How's this ? Did'nt the goat bring the dinner, and give you the message ?" " Goat indeed ! Musha, if you're not the naturals to be made a *gazabo* of by that *cannat* of a Gilla Rua!" They looked at one another. " He's done us," says they. "Let us go and beat him within an inch of his life."

They went to his house with three good saplins in their hands. They heard a great scolding match outside, and when they got in they saw Gilla with a face like fire, *cutting gaaches* (figures) in the air with a carving knife, and Cauth doubled up in a corner afraid of her life. " Eh, man, don't kill the poor woman ; what did she do ?" " She done enough, and more than enough. She put me up to play the rogue on my good neighbours with them goats ; but I'll have her life, so I will." He made a dart at her, and thrust the point of the knife into a white pudding full of blood that she had fixed snug and *sausty* under her arm. Out spouted the blood, down fell Cauth, and lay as stiff as a stake after a kick or two.

"Oh gracious !" says Gilla, coming to himself, "what's this I've done ? took your life, my poor woman, for nothing as I might say. Oh, I'll be hung as high as *Gildheroy*, and I deserve it. Oh ! *Vuya, Vuya,* why was I ever born ? But what am I sayin', and didn't remember my magic fife?" He run to a box, took out a fife, and began to play, "Tatther Jack Walsh" on it, and Cauth was up in two shakes, and dancing like mad. " This is astonishing," says the brothers. They forgot to ask for their twenty guineas, and when they were going home, they were ten more guineas less than when they entered the house, but they had the magic fife with them.

Says Gilla, when he was giving it up, " Till you're used to it, I wouldn't, if I was you, kill any neighbour, or any one of your family. Try your skill on a pig, or a goose, or any beast you'd be after killing, and never fear but you'll be astonished. Well, they thought their heels too slow till they got home. A pig was killed without loss of time, and the eldest fellow began to blow into the fife like vengeance. *Ovoch!* the better he played the stiffer grew the poor carcase, and they began to find they were taken in again.

They came to Gilla's house, but he wasn't to be had. But they watched, and they watched, and they never rested till they had him caught, tied up in a sack, and flung over one of their shoulders. All their intention was to drown him, and put it out of his power to play them more tricks.

They relieved one another, but they were as tired as tired could be when they were passing the "Cat and Bagpipes" within half a quarter of a mile of the deep pool in the river.

"How heavy the thief is!" says the one that was carrying him. Lend a hand, and let us hang the sack on that stump of a bough and get a drink." No sooner said than done, and in with the fellows to refresh themselves.

Just then two men were driving by a flock of sheep, and what did they hear but some one over their heads crying out, "I won't have her; I won't be his son-in-law." They looked up, and there was the voice coming out of the bag. "What are you doing there?" said they, "and who is it you won't marry?" "Sure it's the king's daughter. His servants are drinking now within there, and when they're done they'll carry me to the palace, and put me to death if I don't marry the princess." "And what can we do for you?" "Loosen the cord, let me out, and put one of your sheep inside. I live at *such a place*, and if you come there with me I'll pay you well for the wether." The men did as they were asked, and Gilla and they went on driving the flock.

They were about a mile and a half away, when they saw the three brothers coming after them. "Oh murdher!" says one of them to the others, "there is Gilla, as stout and strong as if he wasn't at the bottom of the turn-hole. What are we to do?" They came up, and Gilla shook hands with them so good naturedly. "Ah, good neighbours," said he, you've just done me the greatest favour in Europe. But you needn't ask me how. I'll not tell you, for it wasn't out of good nature entirely you did the good deed. You see that flock of sheep, these honest men is helping me to drive home. I can get a larger flock any hour or any day I like."

"Oh, faith, we'll take our oaths never to do an ill turn to

you while we live." "Ah, but you might break them." "Oh no, I'll swear by *so and so*, my second brother by *so and so*, and the youngest by *so and so*. No one ever knew us to break one of them oaths."

So they took the oaths, and he then told them that when he was pitched into the water, he went down, down, till at last he came to a meadow with thousands of sheep grazing on it, and that a venerable shepherd gave him leave to bring away all he wanted. "And here they are," said he. "Well, and can't we jump in," said one fellow, "and go down to the meadow?" "It would be no use," said Gilla, "you must be tied in a sack and thrown in; you may get any of your friends to fasten you in sacks and pitch you in." "Oh no, that 'ud be telling the secret and spoil our market. You and these honest men come with us, and pitch us in."

So the sheep were left in a pasture, and the men went back. They got sacks at a farmer's house, and Gilla and the shepherds pretended to tie them up hard and fast when they came to the bank. But they left the cords so that they could be easily loosed, and threw them in where there was hardly five feet of water. Well they could see neither meadows nor sheep, and when they found the breath leaving them, they struggled and opened the mouths of the sacks and got out. Well, they were mad with anger and shame, but they were afraid of breaking their oaths, and that Gilla would play them a worse trick than any of the others. So they did not molest him any more. May every rogue like them fare off as bad!

THE FELLOW IN THE GOAT-SKIN.

The following story is in the main identical with that of *Gilla na Chreckan Gour* in the former series. However, it differs considerably from it in the language and some of the circumstances, besides it enters more into detail. The *Scealuidhe* from whom it has been obtained considers it a more perfect piece of extravagance than the other, but his judgment is not to be relied on, as he prefers a version heard in the morn of life to one he finds in print at an advanced hour of its afternoon. The public are welcome to their own opinions on the subject.

THERE was a poor widow living down there near the Iron Forge when the country was all covered with forests, and you might walk on the tops of trees from Carnew to the Lady's Island, and she had one boy. She was very poor, as I said before, and was not able to buy clothes for her son. So when she was going out, she fixed him snug and *combustible* (comfortable) in the ash-pit, and piled the warm ashes about him. The boy knew no better, and was as happy as the day was long; and he was happier still when a neighbour gave his mother a kid, to keep him company while herself was abroad. The kid and the lad played like two may-boys, and when she was old enough to give milk, wasn't it a god-send to the little family? You wont prevent the boy from growing up into a young man, but not a screed of clothes had he then no more than when he was a gorsoon.

One day as he was sitting comfortably in his pew, he heard poor Jin bleating outside so dismally. It was only one step for him to the door, another to the middle of the road, and another to the gap going into the wood; and there he saw a pack of deer hounds tearing the life out of his poor goat. He snatched a *rampike* out of the gap, was up with the dogs while a cat would be licking her ear, and in two shakes he made *smithereens* of the whole bilin' of them. The hunters spurred their horses to ride him down, but he ran at them with the terrible club, roaring with rage and grief; and horses and men were out of sight before he could wink. He then went back, crying, to the poor goat. Her tongue was hanging out, and her legs quivering, and after she strove to lift her head and lick his hand, she lay down cold and dead.

He lifted the body, and carried it into the cabin, and *pullilued* over it till he fell asleep out of weariness; and then a butcher, that came in with other neighbours to pity him, took away the body, and dressed the skin so smooth and so soft, and fastened two thongs to two of the corners. When the boy's grief was a little mollified, the neighbour stepped in, and fastened the nice skin round his body. It fell to his knees, and the head skin was in front like a Highlander's pocket.

He was so proud of his new dress, that he walked out with his head touching the sky, and up and down the town with him two or three times. "Oh dear!" says the people standing at their doors, and admiring the great big boy, "look at the *Gilla na Chreckan Gour*;" and that name remained on him till he went into his coffin. But pride and fine dress wont make the pot boil. So his mother says to him next morning, "Tom," says she, for that was his real name, "you're idle long enough, so now that you are well clad, and needn't be ashamed to appear before the neighbours, take that rope, and bring in a special good *bresna* [fagot] of rotten boughs from the forest." "Never say it twice," says Gilla, and off he set into the heart of the wood. He broke off and gathered up a great big fagot, and was tying it when he heard a roar that was enough to split an oak, and up walks a *joiant* a foot taller than himself, and he was a foot taller than the tallest man you'd see in a fair.

"What brings you here, you *vagabone*?" says the giant, says he, "*threspassin'* in my demesne, and stealin' my firewood?" "I'm doing no harm," says Gilla, "but clearing your wood, if it is your wood, of rotten boughs." "I'll let you see the harm you're doing," says the giant; and, with that, he made a blow at Gilla, that would have felled an ox. "Is that the way you show civility to your neighbours?" says the other, leaping out of the way of the club: "here's at you;" and he leaped in, and caught the giant by the body, and gave him such a heave that his head came within an inch of the ground. But he was as strong as Goliah, and worked up, and gave Gilla another heave equal to the one he got himself. So they held at it, tripping, squeezing, and twisting, and the hard ground became a bog under their feet, and the bog became like the hard road. At last Gilla gave the giant a great twist, got his right leg behind *his* right leg, and flung him headlong again the root of an oak tree.

He caught up the club from where the giant let it fall at the beginning of the scrimmage, and said to him, "I am going to knock out your brains; what have you to say *again* it ?" "Oh, nothing at all! But if you spare my life, I'll give you a flute that, whenever you play on it, will set your greatest enemies a dancing, and they wont have power to lay their hands on you, if they were as mad as march hares to kill you." "Let us have it," says Gilla, "and take yourself out of that." So the giant handed him the flute out of his oxter-pocket, and home went Gilla as proud as a *paycock*, with his fagot on his back and his flute stuck in it.

In three days time he went to get another fagot; and this day he was attacked by a brother of the same giant; and whatever trouble he had with the other he had it twice with this one. He levelled him at last, and only gave him his life on being offered a bottle of soft green wax of a wonderful nature. If a person only rubbed it on the size of a crown-piece of his body, fire, nor iron, nor any sharp thing could do him the least harm for a year and a day after. Home went Gilla with his bottle, and never stirred out for three days, for he was a little tired and bruised after his wrestling. The next fagot he went to gather, he met with the third brother, and if they had'nt the dreadful struggle, leave it till again! They held at it from noon till night, and then the giant was forced to give in. What he gave for his life was a club, that he took away once from a hermit, and any one fighting with that club in a just cause would never be conquered.

If Gilla staid at home three days after the last struggle, he did'nt stir for a week after this. It was of a Monday morning he got up, and he heard a blowing of bugles, and a terrible hullabulloo in the street. Himself and his mother ran to the door, and there was a fine fat man on horseback, with a jockey's cap on his head, and a quilt with six times the colours of the rainbow on it hanging over his shoulders. "Hear all you good people," says he, after another pull at his bugle horn. "The king of Dublin's daughter has not laughed for three years and a half, and her father promises her in marriage, and his crown after his death, to whoever makes her laugh three times." "And here's the boy," says Gilla, "will make her do that, or know the reason why."

If one was to count all the threads in a coat, it would never come into the tailor's hands, and if I was to reckon all that Gilla's mother and her neighbours said to him before he set out, and all the steps he took after he set out, I'd never have him as far as the gates of Dublin; but to Dublin he got at last, as sure as fate. They were going to stop him at the gates, but he gave a curl of his club round his shoulder, and said he was coming to make the princess laugh. So they laughed, and let him pass; and maybe the doors and windows were not crowded with women and children gazing after the good-natured-looking young giant, with his long black hair falling on his shoulders, and his goat-skin skirt hanging from his waist to his knee. There was a great crowd in the palace yard when he reached there, and ever so many of them playing all sorts of tricks to get a laugh from the princess; but not a smile, even, could be got from her. "What is your business?" said the king, "and where do you come from?" "I come, my liege," said Gilla, "from the country of the "Yellow Bellies," and my business is to make the princess, God bless her! give three hearty laughs." "God enable you!" said the king. But an ugly, cantankerous fellow near the king, with a white face and red hair on him, put in his spoon, and says he to Gilla, "My fine fellow, before any one is allowed to strive for the princess, he is expected to show himself a man at all sorts of matches with the champions of the court." "Nothing will give me greater pleasure," says Gilla. So he laid down his club, and spit in his fists, and a brave sturdy Galloglach came up, and took him by the shoulder and elbow. If he did, he did'nt keep his hold long: Gilla levelled him while you'd wink, and then came another and another, till two score were pitched on their heads.

Well, no one gripped him the second time; but at last all were so mad that they stopped rubbing their heads, and hips, and shoulders, and made at Gilla in a body. The princess was looking very much pleased at Gilla all the time, but now she cried out to her father to stop the attack. The white-faced fellow said something in the king's ear, and not a budge did he make. But Gilla did not let himself be flurried. He took up his *kippeen*, and gave this fellow a tap on his left ear, and that fellow a tap on his right ear, and the other a crack on the ridge pole of his head; and maybe it was'nt a purty spectacle to see every soul of two score of them tumbling *over an' hether*, their heads in the dust, and their heels in the air, and they roaring "Murdher" at the *ling* of their life. But the best of it was that the princess, when she saw the confusion, gave a laugh like the ring of silver on a stone, so sweet and so loud, that all in the court heard it; and Gilla struck his club butt-end on the ground, and says he, "King of Dublin, I have won half of your daughter."

The face of Red-head turned from white to yellow, but no one minded him, and the king invited Gilla to dine with himself and the princess and all the royal family. So that day passed, and while they were at breakfast next morning, Red-head reminded the king that he had nothing to do now but to send the new champion to kill the wild beast, that was murdering every one that attempted to go a hen's race beyond the city walls. The king did not say a word one way or the other, but the princess said it was not right nor kind to send a stranger out to his certain death, for no one ever escaped the wild beast, if it could get near them. "I'll make the trial," says Gilla. "I'd face twenty wild beasts to do any service to yourself or your subjects."

So he inquired where the beast was to be found, and White-face was only too ready to give him his directions. The princess was sorrowful enough, when she saw him setting out, but go he must and would. After he was gone a mile beyond the gates, he heard a terrible roar in the wood and a great cracking of boughs, and out pounced a terrible beast on him, with great long claws, and a big mouth open to swallow him, club and all.

When he was at the very last spring, Gilla gave him a stroke on the nose; and crack! he was sprawling on his back in two seconds. Well, that did not daunt him: he was up, and springing again at Gilla, and this time the blow came on him between the two eyes. Down and up he was again and again, till his right ear, his left ear, his right shoulder, and left shoulder were black and blue.

Then he sat on his hind quarters, and looked very surprised at Gilla and his club. "Now, my tight fellow," says Gilla, "follow your nose to Dublin gates. Do no harm to any one, and I'll do no harm to you." "Waw! waw! waw!" says the beast, with his long teeth all stripped, and sparks flashing from his eyes; but when he saw the club coming down on him, he put his tail between his legs, and walked on. Now and then he'd turn about, and give a growl, but a flourish of the club would soon set him on the straight road again. Oh! if there wasn't racing and tearing into houses and bawns, as they passed through the streets, and roaring and bawling; but Gilla nor the beast ever drew rein till they came to the palace yard.

Well, if the people in the streets were frightened, the people in the court were terrified. The king and his daughter were in a balcony or something that way, and so were out of danger; but lord, and gentleman, and officer, and soldier, as soon as they laid eye on the beast, began to run into passages and halls; but those that got in first shut the doors in their fright; and they that were kept out, did not know what to do; and the king cried out to Gilla to take away the frightful thing. Gilla at once took his flute out of his goat-skin pocket, and began to play, and everyone in the court,—beast and body—began to dance. There was the unfortunate beast obliged to stand on his hind legs, and play heel and toe, while he shovelled about after those that were next him, and he growling fearfully all the time. The people striving to keep out of his way were still obliged to mind their steps, but that didn't prevent them from roaring out to Gilla to free them from their tormentor. The beast kept a steady eye on Red-head, and was always sliding after him as well as the figures of the dance would let him; and you may be sure the poor fellow's teeth were not strong enough to keep his tongue quiet. Well, it was all a fearful thing to look at, but it was very comical too; and as soon as the princess saw that Gilla's power over the beast was strong enough to prevent him from doing any hurt, and especially when she heard the roars of Red-head, and looked at his dancing, she burst out laughing the second time.

"Now, King of Dublin," said Gilla. "I have won two halves of the princess, and I hope it wont be long till the third half will fall to me." "Oh! for goodness' sake," said the king, "never mind halves or quarters: banish this vagabone beast to Bandon, or Halifax, or Lusk, or the Red *Say*, and we'll see what is to come next." Gilla took his flute out of his mouth, and the dancing stopped like shot. The poor beast was thrown off his balance, and fell on his side, and a good many of the dancers had a tumble at the same moment. Then said Gilla to the beast, "You see that street leading straight to the mountain. Down that street with you; don't let a hare catch you; and if you fall, don't wait to get up; and if I ever hear of you coming within a mile of castle or cabin within the four seas of Ireland, I'll make an example of you; remember the club." He had no need to give his orders twice. Before he was done speaking the beast was half way down the street like a frightened dog with a kettle tied to his tail. He was once after seen in the Devil's Glen in Wicklow, picking a bone, and that's all was ever heard of him.

Well, that was work enough for one day, and the potatoes were just done in the big kitchen of the palace. I don't know what great people take instead of stirabout and milk before they go to bed. Indeed people do be saying that some of them never leave the table from dinner to bed-time, but I don't believe it. Anyhow they took dinner and supper, and went to bed, everything in its own time, and rose in the morning when the sun was as high as the trees.

So when they were at breakfast, Red-head, who wasn't at all agreeable to the match, says to the King in Gilla's hearing: "The Danes, ill luck be in their road! will be near the city in a day or two; and it is said in an old prophecy book, that if you could get the flail that's hanging on the couple under the ridge pole of Hell you could drive every enemy you have into the sea,—Dane or divel. I'm sure, sir, Gilla wouldn't have much trouble in getting that flail: nothing seems too hot or too heavy for him." "If he goes," said the princess, "it is against my wish and will." "If he goes," said the King, "it is not by my order." "Go I will," said Gilla, "if any one shows me the way." There was an old gentleman with a red nose on him sitting at the table, and says he, "Oh! I'll shew you the way: it lies down Cut Purse Row. You will know it by the sign of the "Cat and Bagpipes" on one side, and the "Ace of Spades" stuck in the window opposite." "I'm off," says Gilla: "pray all of you for my safe return." He easily found the "Cat and Bag-pipes," and the "Ace of Spades," and nothing further is said of him till he was knocking at Hell's Gate.

It was opened by an old fellow with horns on him seven feet long, and says he to Gilla, mighty politely, "What is it you want here, sir?" "I am a great traveller," said Gilla, "and wish to see every place worth seeing, inside and outside." "Oh! if that's the case," says the porter, "walk in. Here, brothers, show this gentleman-traveller all the curosities of the place." With that they all, big and little, locked and bolted every window and door, and stuffed every hole, till a midge itself couldn't find its way out; and then they surrounded Gilla with their spits, and pitch-forks, and *sprongs*; and if they didn't whack and prod him it's a wonder. "Gentlemen," says Gilla, "these are the tricks of clowns. Fair play is bonny play: show yourselves gentlemen if you have a good drop at all in you. Hand me a weapon, and let us fight fair. There's an old flail on that couple, it will do as well as another." "Oh, yes! the flail! the flail!" cried *them* all; and some little imps climbed up the rafters, pulled down the flail, and handed it to Gilla, expecting to see his hands burned through the moment it touched them.. They knew nothing of the giant's balsam that Gilla rubbed on his hands as he was coming along, but they soon knew and felt the strength of his arm when he was knocking them down like nine-pins, and thrashing them, arms, legs, and bodies, like so much oaten straw. "Oh! murdher! murdher!" says the big devil of all, at last. "Stop your hand, and we'll give you anything in our power." "Well," says Gilla, "I've seen all I want in your habitation. I don't like the welcome I've got, and will thank you to open the gate." Oh! wasn't there twenty pair of legs tearing in a moment to let Gilla out. "You don't mean, I hope, to carry off the flail," says the big fellow; "it's very useful to us in winter." "It was the very thing that brought me here," says Gilla, "to get it, and I won't leave without it; but if you look in the black pool of the Liffey at noon to-morrow, you'll find it there." Well, they were very down in the mouth for the loss of the flail, but a second rib-roasting wasn't to be thought of. When they had him fairly locked out, they put out their tongues at him through the bars, and shouted, "Ah! Gilla na Chreckan Gour! wait till you're let in here so easy again;" but he only answered, "You'll let me in when I ask you."

There was both joy and terror at court when they saw Gilla coming back with the terrible flail in his hand. "Now," says every one, "we care little for the Danes and all their kith and kin. But how did you coax the fellows down below to give up the implement?" So he told them as much as he chose, and was very glad to see the welcome that was on the princess's face. Red-head thought it would be a fine thing to have the flail in his power. So he crept over to where Gilla laid it aside after charging no one to touch it; but his hand did not come within a foot of it, when he thought it was burned to the bone. He danced about, shook his arm, put his fist to his mouth, and roared out for water. "Couldn't you mind what I said?" says Gilla, "and that wouldn't have happened." However he took Red-head's hand within his own two that had the ointment, and he was freed from the burning at once. Well, the poor rogue looked so relieved, and so ashamed, and so impudent at the same time, that the princess joined in the laughing of all about. "Three halves at last," said Gilla. "Now, my liege," said he, "I hope that after I give a good throuncing to the Danes, you will fulfil your promise." "There are no two ways about that," said the king. "Danes or no Danes, you may marry my daughter to-morrow, if she makes no objection herself." Red-head, seeing by the princess's face that she wasn't a bit vexed at what her father said, ran up to his room, thrust his head into a cupboard, and nearly roared his arm off, but the company down stairs did not seem to miss him.

Early in the forenoon of next day a soldier came running in all haste from the bridge that crossed the Liffey, and said the Danes were coming in thousands from the north, all in brass armour, brass pots on their heads, and brass pot-lids on their arms, and that the yellow blaze coming from their ranks was enough to blind a body. Out marched the king's troops with the king at their head, to hinder the Danes from getting into the town over the bridge. First went Gilla with his flail in one hand, and his club in the other. He crossed the bridge, and when the enemy were about ten perch away from him, he shouted out, "This flail belongs to the devil, and who has a better right to it than his children?" So saying, he swung it round his head, and flung it with all his power at the front rank. It mowed down every man it met in its course, and when it cut through the whole column, and the space was clear before it, it sunk down, and flame and smoke flew up from the breach it made in the ground. The soldiers at each side of the lane of dead men ran forward on Gilla, but as every one came within the sweep of his club, he was dashed down on the bridge or into the river. On they rushed like a snow storm, but they melted like the same snow falling into a furnace. Gilla kept before the pile of the dead soldiers, but at last his arms began to tire. Then the king and his men came over, and the rest of the Danes were frightened and fled.

Often was Gilla tired in his past life, but that was the greatest and tiresomest exploit he ever done. He lay on a settle bed for three days; but if he did, hadn't he the princess and all her maids of honour to wait on him, and pity him, and give him gruel, and toast, and tay of all the colours under the sun.

Redhead did his best to stop the marriage, but once when he was speaking to the king, one of the body guards swore he'd open his skull with his battle-axe if ever he dared open his mouth again about it. So married they were, and as strong as Gilla was, if ever his princess and himself had a *scruting* [dispute], I know who got the upper hand.

THE HAUGHTY PRINCESS.

THERE was once a very worthy king, whose daughter was the greatest beauty that could be seen far or near, but she was as proud as Lucifer, and no king or prince would she agree to marry. Her father was tired out at last, and invited every king, and prince, and duke, and earl that he knew or didn't know to come to his court to give her one trial more. They all came, and next day after breakfast they stood in a row in the lawn, and the princess walked along in the front of them to make her choice. One was fat, and says she, "I won't have you, Beer-barrel!" One was tall and thin, and to him she said, "I won't have you, Ramrod!" To a white-faced man she said, "I won't have you, Pale Death;" and to a red-cheeked man she said, "I won't have you, Cockscomb!" She stopped a little before the last of all, for he was a fine man in face and form. She wanted to find some defect in him, but he had nothing remarkable but a ring of brown curling hair under his chin. She admired him a little, and then carried it off with, "I won't have you, Whiskers!"

So all went away, and the king was so vexed, he said to her, "Now, to punish your *impedence*, I'll give you to the first beggarman or singing *sthronshuch* that calls," and, as sure as the hearth-money, a fellow all over rags, and hair that came to his shoulders, and a bushy red beard all over his face, came next morning, and began to sing before the parlour window.

When the song was over, the hall-door was opened, the singer asked in, the priest brought, and the princess married to Beardy. She roared and she bawled, but her father didn't mind her. "There," says he to the bridegroom, "is five guineas for you. Take your wife out of my sight, and never let me lay eyes on you or her again."

Off he led her, and dismal enough she was. The only thing that gave her relief was the tones of her husband's voice and his genteel manners. "Whose wood is this?" said she, as they were going through one. "It belongs to the king you called Whiskers yesterday." He gave her the same answer about meadows and corn fields, and at last a fine city. "Ah, what a fool I was!" said she to herself. "He was a fine man, and I might have him for a husband." At last they were coming up to a poor cabin, "Why are you bringing me here?" says the poor lady. "This was my house," said he, "and now it's yours." She began to cry, but she was tired and hungry, and she went in with him.

Ovoch! there was neither a table laid out, nor a fire burning, and she was obliged to help her husband to light it, and boil their dinner, and clean up the place after; and next day he made her put on a stuff gown and a cotton handkerchief. When she had her house readied up, and no business to keep her employed, he brought home *sallies* [willows], peeled them, and showed her how to make baskets. But the hard twigs bruised her delicate fingers, and she began to cry. Well, then he asked her to mend their clothes, but the needle drew blood from her fingers, and she cried again. He couldn't bear to see her tears, so he bought a creel of earthenware, and sent her to the market to sell them. This was the hardest trial of all, but she looked so handsome and sorrowful, and had such a nice air about her, that all her pans, and jugs, and plates, and dishes were gone before noon, and the only mark of her old pride she showed was a slap she gave a buckeen across the face when he *axed* her to go in an' take share of a quart.

Well, her husband was so glad, he sent her with another creel the next day, but faith, her luck was after deserting her. A drunken huntsman came up riding, and his beast got in among her ware, and made *brishe* of every mother's son of 'em. She went home cryin', and her husband wasn't at all pleased. "I see," said he, "you're not fit for business. Come along, I'll get you a kitchen-maid's place in the palace. I know the cook."

So the poor thing was obliged to stifle her pride once more. She was kept very busy, and the footman and the butler would be very impudent about looking for a kiss, but she let a screech out of her the first attempt was made, and the cook gave the fellow such a lambasting with the besom that he made no second offer. She went home to her husband every night, and she carried broken victuals wrapped in papers in her side pockets.

A week after she got service there was great bustle in the kitchen. The king was going to be married, but no one knew who the bride was to be. Well, in the evening the cook filled the princess's pockets with cold meat and puddings, and says she, "Before you go, let us have a look at the great doings in the big parlour." So they came near the door to get a peep, and who should come out but the king himself, as handsome as you please, and no other but King Whiskers himself. "Your handsome helper must pay for her peeping," says he to the cook, "and dance a jig with me." Whether she would or no, he held her hand and brought her into the parlour. The fiddlers struck up, and away went *him* and *her*. But they hadn't danced two steps when the meat and the *puddens* flew out of her pockets. Every one roared out, and she flew to the door, crying piteously. But she was soon caught by the king, and taken into the back parlour. "Don't you know me, my darling?" said he. "I'm both King Whiskers, your husband the ballad singer, and the drunken huntsman. Your father knew me well enough when he gave you to me, and all was to drive your pride out of you." Well, she didn't know how she was with fright, and shame, and joy. Love was uppermost anyhow, for she laid her head on her husband's breast and cried like a child. The maids of honour soon had her away and dressed her as fine as hands and pins could do it; and there were her mother and father, too; and while the company were wondering what end of the handsome girl and the king, he and his queen, *who* they didn't know in her fine clothes, and the other king and queen came in, and such rejoicings and fine doings as there was, none of us will ever see, any way.

DOCTOR CURE-ALL.

THERE was once a poor fagot-cutter that used to work very hard, and one day that he took a load of fagots to the doctor in the next town, he was brought into the parlour to be paid, and didn't he admire the fine furniture he saw about him! When he was coming away, says he to the doctor, "Musha, sir, would you lend me one of these fine-bound books for about a quarter of a year or so, and I'll return it honestly?" "What is the book to be about?" says the doctor, "and what do you want with it?" "I don't care what it's about," says he, "and I'll tell you when I return it the use I'll make of it." The doctor laughed, and gave him a well-looking *wolume*, but I don't know no more nor the fagot-cutter himself what was in it.

"A fine thing," says he, "to be slavin' oneself as I do for my bit and sup, and see what grandeur that man is in for doing nothing at all, as a body might say." When he got home, he removed bag and baggage into the town after selling his little furniture, and buying a *shute* of broadcloth, and a *Caroline* hat, and a Barcelona *hankecher*. He got a painter to put up a sign-board with DOCTOR CURE-ALL over his door, put some bottles on a shelf, and sat down at his little round table with his book before him. Well, he soon got custom, but all the cures he knew was *bowl almanac* [Bole-Armeniac], salts and senna, castor oil, and sugar and soap for plasters. But he was so courageous in promising cures, and so many got well, no thanks to him, and there was so many that there was nothing amiss with at all, that he soon got a great name. He even recovered stolen things, for he gave out that he knew by his books who had them, and the thieves used to bring them unknownst to him, and give him some money for not telling on them.

Well, there was a gentleman in the neighbourhood that had a very valuable ring taken from him, and he sent for Dr. Cure-all to find out the thief for him. "I'll find him out," says he, "if he's above ground, but it can't be done in a minute. I'll have to see where you kept it, and get a lock of hair from every one in the house, and study my conjurin' book for eight days. The ninth morning you'll have the ring safe and sound. I'll have to stay on the premises the whole time." "Very good," says the gentleman.

Well, he lived like a fighting cock for five days, but I give you my word he began then to get uneasy, for no one about the house seemed inclined to confess, though he gave out from the beginning that he'd have his hand on the thief the evening of the eighth day. The evening of the sixth he was walking in the paddock near the hedge, and he was muttering to himself, "Three days only now, and be this and be that there goes one of 'em!" says he in an angry voice. Well, there was three rogues of servants concerned in the robbery, and one of them was *padrowlin'* [patrolling] in the cabbage-garden the other side of the hedge the same minute. He never drew rein till he got to the other fellows, and says he, "We're discovered as sure as fate."

Well, they talked and they talked, and didn't know what to do till next evening, when the second of 'em was close by the hedge, and what did he hear but the doctor cry out, "And there goes the second of 'em!" Well, they were more frightened now than before, and came to the point of confessing if the doctor knew there was three of 'em. The next evening the poor man was walking sorrowful enough in the same place. "Ovoch!" was he saying to himself, "there was only three evenings of the time left since I took my walk here to give the thief an opportunity of talking to me," and then his heart was so bitter he cried out, "Here is the third of 'em!" "Docthor, docthor," says a voice the other side of the hedge, "you're a considherate man; here's the ring and a guinea-note along with it: keep our secret." "You don't deserve it, you unlucky rogue, for delaying so long. The master 'ud have you in the *stone-jug* [gaol] to-morrow only for your late repentance."

Well, the whole family were assembled in the big parlour next morning, and the doctor sitting very stately in an arm-chair. "Who is the robber?" says the master. "I know the robber, and the place he hid the ring," says the doctor, "but I can only reveal one; which is it to be?" The master, of course, chose to get his valuable ring. "Well, then," says he, "go to the hen-house wherever that is; I don't know. Put your right hand on the little board that's inside over the door, and in the middle of it you'll find what you're in search of." Out went the mistress and the little girl that minded the fowl, and there the ring was sure enough.

Well, there was great joy, you may depend, and very

great honour was paid to the wise man, but the master's brother that came that day on a visit, wouldn't give the doctor any credit at all. "Wait till dinner time," says he "and if I don't astonish his weak mind, you may say what you like." Well, the brother and his servant were cooking something very secretly in the kitchen before dinner time, and when that was over, and the doctor's health was drunk, and himself greatly praised, says the brother, "Doctor, I'll praise you more than all the family if you tell me what's in this covered plate." Ah, wouldn't anyone pity the poor man at that moment? "No use," says he to himself, " in throwing sand in people's eyes any longer." Then speaking out loud, says he, "Ah, sir, let the fox go as far as he pleases, he'll be *cotch* [caught] at last." "Well," says the gentleman, "I see I must give it up. It's a bit of a fox sure enough!" He lifted the cover for an instant, and then threw plate and cover and fox out of the window. And that's the way with the world. *Impedence* will bring a man through an auger hole, where an honest man can't get through an open gate.

THE WISE MEN OF GOTHAM.

THERE was once a townland called Gotham, but maybe it's now swallowed up and covered with sand like Bannow, or maybe a moving bog went over it, for I never heard any one say he knew where it was. Well, four brothers lived in it, and they were called the wise men of Gotham, and you might as well call Pat Neil [see "*The Banks of the Boro*"] a wise man, I'm sure. One of them took a big cheese to town to sell it one market day. He was on horseback, and just as he came to the brow of a steep hill just outside the town, the cheese dropped and began to roll down the slope like vengeance. "Oh, ho!" says he, "is that the way? I'll take this other road into town, and I'll engage I'll get there before you." So he put spurs to his horse, and he was soon in the nighest street that was just at the bottom of the hill. Neither the cheese nor the ghost of the cheese was there. He rode up the hill, and looked in the dykes for his cheese, but, 'deed, he returned home hungry and dry, and he had neither the cheese nor the value of it.

Well, they were blaming him, sure enough, till he began to think he hadn't done a very wise thing after all. "And what would you do if you were in my place?" said he to one of his brothers. "Well, I think I'd go and buy another cheese the same size and roll it down, and ride after it and see where it would go." "That's not a bad thought," says another, "but if it happened to me I think I'd sit at the market-cross till I'd hear the bell-man crying out where it was to be got, for it's very likely some honest person found it." "But," says the last, "I think I'd pay Browzy [the once bellman of Enniscorthy] a thirteen to cry it, and offer half of it for reward. For didn't yez all often hear, " Half a loaf is better than no bread?"

Next market day another of the brothers went to sell another cheese, and he determined he'd be very cunning if any mischance happened him. Well, just at the very same place he dropped his cheese too. It didn't roll, for it came down in a car-track. This second wise man pulled out his sword, and made a prod at it to lift it up, but it was too short, and if it was long enough itself, it was too blunt at the end. So he rode into the town, and bought a long sword with a sharp point at the cutler's, and rode back again.

His cheese wasn't there, nor half way down the hill, nor at the bottom of the hill. He recollected what was said at home, and sat at the market cross till sunset to see if the honest finder would cry it. Then he paid his thirteen to the bellman, offering half the cheese to the finder for reward. But the poor man had the dark night round him coming home, and no great welcome when he got there, for he had neither the cheese nor its value no more than his brother.

The four brothers cared for no one's company but their own, and they all lived together. But a neighbour who had a few marriageable daughters said so much about what a shame it was for none of them to have a wife, that a match was made up between the eldest and the neighbour's eldest daughter, and a new house was built for the couple at the end of the big bawn. The evening before the wedding, says the bridegroom, "I'm rather afeard of this change. I've heard of women tyrannizing over their husbands, and beating them within an inch of their lives, and if she took a fancy to throunce me in the night, you wouldn't hear me from the new house." That speech frightened the whole family. "Ah!" says the second eldest, "let it be put in the marriage articles that there shan't be a stick kept in the house thicker than your little finger. She can't kill you with that, anyway." Well, that gave them all great comfort, till a *gomula* of a servant-boy put in his word. "Oh, faith, if she's inclined for battle it's not the little kippeen she'll take to, while she has the tongs at hand." All were thrown into a quandary again, but the boy soon gave them relief. "I'll tell you what we'll do. When the new mistress, God bless her, goes to whack the young master, let him bawl out like a man. The boy 'ill hear him from the stable loft, he'll bawl out, and the thresher will hear him from his *shass* [heap of sheaves] in the barn. I'll hear the thresher from the settle-bed in the kitchen. The old mistress 'll hear me, and all the house 'll hear her." They all clapped their hands for joy, and the marriage didn't frighten anyone. The stable boy, and the thresher, and the boy in the settle said they didn't close an eye for a whole week after the marriage, for fear of an attack on the master. I don't believe them. No one staid awake after that, and the bridegroom might be killed for anything they *done* to hinder it.

At last all were married to the other sisters, but the dickens a foot farther than the four corners of the big bawn they'd separate from one another.

They were all conversing one day in the bawn, and one of them made a remark that put them all into a great fright. "Aren't there four brothers of us altogether?" says he. "To be sure," says one, and "To be sure," says another. "Well," says he, "I'm after counting, and I can't make out one more than three." "And neither can I," says one, and "Neither can I," says another, and "Neither can I," says the last. "Some one must be dead or gone away." Well, they were all in a fright, I can tell you, for a while. At last says the one that spoke first, "Let every one go and sit on the ridge of his house, and I'll soon see who is missing." Well, they done so, and then the poor fellow that staid to count, after looking all round, cried out, "Oh, murdher, murdher! there's no one on my own house. It's myself that's missing." That's all I ever heard of the Wise Men of Gotham, and I'm sure it's no great loss.

THE GOOD BOY AND THE BOY THAT ENVIED HIM.

There was once a lord and lady, and they had two servant boys. One was a fine innocent young fellow that everybody was fond of; the other was an envious ounkrawn, that begrudged all the people about him the very air they breathed. The lady was very kind to the good young boy, because he was so well disposed, and because her little son and daughter were so fond of him. The bad boy was always striving to buz into the lord's head some mistrust of his comrade; and at last, as they were coming home from hunting, a devilish grin came on his face as he pointed to where the lady was standing in the garden, and the page holding her hand in his own two, and his mouth down on it. Well, the lord was astonished you may be sure, and his face became like a coal. He said nothing, but walked up to his room without speaking to any one.

There was a foundry on his estate, and there he rode in the cool of the evening. He went into the room where the great furnace was, and said he to the two men that were minding it, "If any one comes to you to-morrow morning and asks you from me if the job I gave you is done, take him and pitch him into the red fire before you." "Oh Lord, sir, what has he done?" "If he wasn't worthy of death I wouldn't be here to give this order." "Oh, your lordship, it shall be done."

Next morning says he to the young boy, "Go down to the foundry, and ask the two men that are minding the fire if the job I bade them do is finished." The page wished for nothing better. The sun was shining, and he'd have a delightful walk through the meadows and the wood. So he went on, the birds singing in the trees, and he singing along with them out of innocence and a light heart. The meadows brought him to the wood, and he had to go more than two miles across it to come out on the road the other side, and there was the foundry. After he was half a mile into it, he bethought him of an advice his mother gave him when he was leaving home, and that was, never to take a short cut while he had the high road to travel by.

Back he turned to where a cross path led out to the road on his left. About the time he got out on the road, his wicked comrade was entering the wood by the same way himself was taking at first. He kept walking along pretty smart, but not so smart as to overtake the good boy if he hadn't turned back.

While the good boy was going along without hurrying himself, he came up to a little chapel by the roadside, and he did not pass it without going in to say some prayers. For that was another parting advice his mother gave him, never to pass by a chapel that was open without going in and performing some devotion. Mass was just beginning, and he thought for the short time it would hold it wasn't worth his while to go out. So he joined piously with the priest, and when it was over he stepped out rather quick to make up for the delay. When he came to the furnace he asked the men if the job their lord gave them was done. "Oh, faith it is so," said the wickedest-looking of the two, and he put the devil's own grin on him, and pointed to the furnace. Though he didn't understand him, he didn't like his looks nor his tones; so he turned round, and set off as smart as he could home.

The lord was sitting in his hall, rather troubled in mind, and there he had been from soon after the young boy left the house. He began to be afraid that he'd been too hasty. It might be all innocent enough, he thought; my wife might be after doing something for himself or his mother, and that's the way he was showing his gratitude. I was very wrong. There is no more than suspicion after all. He called the first servant that was passing. "Go and tell *So-and-so* [naming the wicked boy]"—— "Sir, I saw him going the same way that the widow's son took after you gave him some directions." "How long after?" "About half an hour." Just at the moment in came the lady of the house, and she made a sign to the servant to go out.

She then held her hand that had a scar on it over to her husband, and said with such a pious and grateful air on her features, "Oh, my dear husband, how happy I am, and how glad you'll be to hear of the escape I had yesterday! While myself, and the children, and the widow's son were walking in the garden, I was pulling a flower, and a snake darted on my hand and bit it. Oh, so frightened as I was! But the poor boy ran and caught it, and sucked away at the wound, spitting out every now and then. The doctor was luckily in the castle, and the moment I could get my hand from the poor boy's mouth, and get to my room, I had him brought. Well, he said nothing could be better than what the poor child did; but, to make sure, he put some caustic to it. He said he couldn't be sure whether there would be any danger till to-day. I did not tell you all along for fear of afflicting you; but the doctor saw it just now, and said there was no danger whatever. Oh, aren't you glad?"

I nor no one could describe the torment the lord endured while his wife was speaking. His face was frightful to see. When his lady stopped he sprung up like a madman and was rushing out, when the door opened and there was the boy he thought burned to a cinder, full of life and sprightliness, before him, and his face so rosy after his walk. Only there was a chair at hand he'd have fallen on the floor. There he sat without saying a word or raising his eyes for a quarter of an hour, feeling a deadly sickness inside, and as if his brain was going to burst. His lady and the page were terribly frightened; but he made signs to them to be quiet, and at last came to himself.

When he was able to question the young boy, and heard all he could tell, and saw no sign of the envious creature making his appearance, he guessed how it came about, and saw the hand of God in the rescue of the innocent and the punishment of the guilty.

He was up to this time a passionate and selfish sort of man, fond of worldly pleasures of all kinds; but a great reformation took place in him from that day. He acknowledged to his wife the whole thing from beginning to end, and while he lived he lamented the doom of the unhappy informer.

CHOOSING THE LEAST OF THREE EVILS.

THERE was once a very holy monk, and the devil was laying siege to him night and day to make him commit sin. Well, the Old Boy was not able to get any advantage over him, but the poor man was tormented out of his life by the constant annoyance he got from the bad thoughts the devil was putting in his head. At last says the black thief to him, "I'll make a bargain with you that you'll own is entirely to your own profit. Commit one mortal sin to oblige me, and I'll let you alone all the rest of your life. And I'll give you your choice. Get drunk, or commit murder, or take liberties with your neighbour's wife." Well, the good man said to himself, "It is better to be left at peace. I'll get drunk; it is much the least of these sins, and sure I'll repent heartily for it, and do penance. What signifies it towards the torment the thief makes me endure putting nasty things in my head every minute in the day?" So in the evening he got his whiskey, and his sugar, and his hot water, and made himself comfortable, and, bedad, he began to indulge in bad thoughts that he'd drive away, with God's help, at any other time the moment they'd enter his head. The porter's wife just came in to stir the fire, or to do something, and nothing would do my poor monk but to fling his arms round her neck and give her a smack. She bawled out, and her husband that was in the passage ran in, and knocked the drunken man down. The devil gave him strength, I suppose, for he got hold of the tongs and gave the husband such a crack on the head as left him senseless. The cries of the woman brought a lot of people into the room, and my poor sinner was taken and punished. I don't know whether the husband was killed or not; but you see by this that we're never to listen to the devil's advice in anything, or commit a sin with our free will for any consideration in the world. The poor monk thought he'd only get drunk, and do nobody any harm, and see the other crimes it brought on his head.

THE HERMIT AND THE ROBBER.

THERE was once a very holy hermit, who was very exact in all his duties; but one cold winter's night, when he was examining his conscience, he recollected that some of his duties of that very day were neglected. He felt such sorrow for his fault that he threw off his clothes, and went into a deep part of the river that ran at the bottom of the hill in which his cell was scooped out. While he was there shivering and perishing with the cold, though he hardly felt it on account of his sorrow, he heard a voice saying, "Come out of the water when this twig blossoms," and at the same time he felt it in his hand. Just then a man went by driving four or five head of cattle before him. When he saw the poor man with only his head above the water, he called out, "Oh, God help you, my poor fellow! can you come near the edge till I pull you out?" "I dont want to be pulled out. I am here punishing myself for a sin of omission." "Omission! what's that? Killed any body after robbing him?" "No." "Betrayed your comrade, and got him hanged?" "No." "Well, robbed a chapel?" &c., &c. "No." "Well, I am beat. What was it then?" "It was so and so;—neglected my prayers, and the few I said were not said with any devotion."

The man was going to laugh, but he stopped himself. "Oh gracious! If you think you deserve punishment for such a fleabite as that, what's to become of me that's just after stealing these cattle, and didn't do much better for seven years past? I'll repent and punish myself just as you're doing. Maybe God will pardon me, when he sees my heart changed." He turned the cattle about, and put them on the way back to their farm, and came back, and stripped himself, and went and stood by the hermit. After some time he heard the same voice, and found the second twig in his hand. Angels appeared to them at last, and the robber was delighted to see blossoms on his twig. He did not see any on the hermit's, and was unwilling to leave the water before him. However it bloomed out half a minute later, and out came the both joyfully. So you see a great sinner that gets a strong turn at once against his evil life, and forsakes it, is in a better state than a shilly-shally lukewarm person, that performs his duties and devotions in a dawdling lazy manner.

BIRTH AND BAPTISM OF ST. MOGUE.

SAINT KILLIAN, on a day of the days missed his oxen which he pastured at Fenagh in Cavan, and set off in quest of them. He came up with them on the edge of Templeport lake, standing without a stir, and looking steadfastly at the island which lay in the middle of the sheet of water. The ferryman's house was near the spot, and he asked the wife if anything remarkable had happened in the island during the night. She said that a strange woman had got herself ferried across to it, and had been delivered of a fine man child. Moreover the bedpost which she had grasped in her pains had sent roots into the ground; and from its top had sprung branches in full leaf and flower, and gone through the roof. "Where's your husband and the boat?" said the saint. "At the farther side of the lake," said she. "Bring out something, on which you may go across to the island for the infant, that I may baptise him." "There is nothing on which I could sit or stand but the hearthstone, and sure that would not do." "Well, try it." "But sure I couldn't lift it." "Make the attempt." She did so, and the flag was no heavier than a thin dry board. The saint placed it on the water, bade the woman get on it, and spread out her shawl to catch the breeze. She obeyed, and had a delightful sail to the island.

There she received the child from Eithne its mother, brought it to the saint, and he baptised it by the name of Mogue. The woman then re-conveyed it to the island to its mother, and in time he became a priest, spent some time with St. David in Wales, and during the later years of his life governed the Bishopric of Ferns in Wexford.

The miraculous hearthstone afterwards conveyed many a corpse to its place of interment in the island.

THE GREEDY MASON.

A SAINT was busily occupied raising the walls of a Cathedral in Ulster; and in order that his workmen should be freed from the annoyance of providing themselves with food, and so have their minds entirely fixed on the great work in hand, his pet cow was slaughtered every evening, carefully skinned, and her flesh cooked for the supper of his people. On this and some bread and sorrel they made a hearty meal, and felt neither hunger nor weariness till their next day's work was done. All the company had charge not to break or injure a bone of the animal: these were collected after the meal, and wrapped carefully in the skin, and next morning the wonderful cow was grazing as composedly as if no liberties had been taken with her fat or lean the evening before.

All this had pleasantly gone on for months, and the building was near its completion, when what should meet the eyes of the saint one morning, as he was going to inspect the progress of the building, but his poor cow limping along on three legs? She lowed dismally at her kind master, and he experienced as sharp a pang of annoyance as any saint could endure. He had the work suspended, and ordered the men all into his presence. "I shall not give any of you," said he, "a pretence for telling a falsehood: pass before me till I discover the sensual wretch who, for sake of a little marrow, broke a leg bone of our poor pet cow, our support, our earthly treasure. Pass before me one by one. I shall soon read in the glutton's face the evidence of his crime.

"No need," said the repentant culprit. "I am the wretch, and will patiently suffer any punishment you may inflict."

"You have done well," said the saint. "Had you endeavoured to conceal your crime, you would die by the fall of a stone before the building would be completed. However, the curse shall remain in your family; and a late descendant of yours shall perish as he passes by this cathedral, from a slipping of one of the walls." To this day a descendant of the man will not dare to walk by the crumbling walls of the old building.

This saintly legend was not the work of an ordinary hagiographer. Some bardic romancer had received by tradition such a pagan myth as that of the Norse deities feeding on their boar or their horse *Sleipner* after their daily combats were ended, and tacked it to the memory of the christian saint.

THE MUSIC OF HEAVEN.

THERE was a monastery once, and it had a nice garden, and between the garden and a big forest there was only a railing that had a door in the middle of it. A very pious monk was sitting in the summer house of the garden one evening, after saying all his prayers and his offices, and he was pondering over different things in the psalms he was after reading, and among the rest one saying that a thousand years was in the sight of God only as a day. He pondered, and he pondered, and he could not understand the words at all, and while he was this way, a bird began to sing in one of the trees just outside the garden. He never heard anything like it in his life before, and it was just what he supposed the melody made by angels to be. At last the bird fluttered away to a tree further off, and the monk went outside of the garden, not to lose any of the notes, and still the bird moved further off, and still the monk followed it, his whole soul and mind and memory all wrapt up in the sweet music. He went into the wood about a quarter of a mile, and he was as he thought about half an hour moving that far, and he couldn't fancy heaven itself to have anything more heavenly than the notes of the bird.

At last it stopped singing, and the poor man felt like one just falling down on the earth out of Paradise. He went back dismally, and when he came to where the paling and the little door in it ought to be, there was a high wall, and towers, and a big door, and a little one beside it. "Oh dear!" said the poor man, "am I dreaming, or what has come over me?" He rang the bell and the little door was opened. "What is your business?" said the porter, a man with a face and dress on him quite strange to the monk. "My business, brother, is to go in, and say my prayers, and go to bed." "Go to bed! You speak as if you belonged to the place, and you a perfect stranger. Who are you?" "Rather you tell me who are you? There was a garden here half an hour ago, when I left it to follow a bird that was singing heavenly music into the wood, and here I find walls and gates where there was a paling between the garden and the wood, and a strange porter, for I don't remember ever seeing your face before." Well, some of the brothers that were going by, gathered round, and could make no more of the business than the porter. They asked him who was the abbot when he left the garden, and what king reigned in the country, and shook their heads when he mentioned their names. They thought they were speaking with a man out of his mind, till at last one of them said, "Let us bring him to Brother *So-and-so*. He's a hundred and ten years old, and maybe he'll help us in our puzzle." They brought him to the old brother through passages and rooms he never saw before, they wondering at his strange dress and he at theirs.

When the old, old man heard the story, he began to speak. "Brothers, when I entered this monastery very young, I often heard from an old brother, who was then as old as I am now, that when himself was a novice the oldest of the monks used to be telling of a brother *So-and-so* that left the house one evening, and never was heard of again." "I am that poor lost brother," said the monk, "and God has thus made me feel how a thousand years in His sight are only as a day, a thing I was striving to understand that evening. A thousand years listening to that bird of heaven would not seem an hour to me. I have now lived centuries beyond my time. Let me make my confession and receive the last sacraments, for I think no further time will be allotted me on earth." And it was so; he died the death of the saints that night.

The fairies are considered by archæologists as the heirs and descendants of the inferior pagan divinities, good and evil. The demi-gods and demons were reduced to this condition when heathenism was outwardly brought to an end. However, the popular belief is that the fairies were those angels who, at Lucifer's revolt, did not openly join him, but felt a kind of sympathy with his wicked aspirations. When the rebel angels were precipitated into hell, these cowardly spirits fell no farther than the earth, on which they are to remain till the day of judgment, uncertain during the whole time whether they are to be pardoned or condemned. Our own Irish fairies are the spirits of the Danaan Druid chiefs, who, after their death, took possession of the chief subterranean caverns throughout the kingdom, and continued, according to their good or evil dispositions, to succour or injure the descendants of the Milesians by whom they had been dispossessed. For further information on the subject of the fairy kingdom the reader is referred to the *Legendary Fictions of the Irish Celts;* Macmillan, 1866. (page 109)

HOW DONN FIRINNE GOT HIS HORSE SHOD.

THE oldest Sighe-Chief of the Milesian line is *Donn Firinne*, the truth-telling king. He was the son of Milé, or Milesius, and when the Danaans raised a fog round the island, to prevent the landing of him and his brothers Heber, Heremon, and Amhergin, he was shipwrecked on the Duchains, in West Munster, and there perished as to his mortal part. The people to this day call these rocks *Teach Duin* (Donn's House). He bestows his attention on the invisible concerns of the whole kingdom, but resides in Knocfierna, near Limerick, and when not presiding over the sumptuous entertainments there furnished, he looks after the fairy tribes of Thomond (North Munster) and Ormond, and occasionally makes a raid at their head against the fairies of Connaught, or Leinster, or South Munster. He is rather patriotic, and friendly besides to native talent. In Croker's Legends is given an address made to him by a poor poet, whose verses seemed to be in no request by king or chief of mortal mould. It begins thus:—

" Donn of the ocean vats, I give due reverence to thee."

Donn would not be a genuine Milesian spirit if ungifted with combative propensities. A blacksmith near the Feale was one night wakened up to put a shoe on the steed of a noble-looking rider. He fashioned it without much delay, but the great feat was to adjust and fasten it on. So skittish and mettlesome were the mare's capers, that he could not bring the iron convenience within a yard of its appointed place. The master, after looking on for some time, with grim amusement playing over his features, quietly wrung off the lower portion of the leg, and presented it to the operator. Awe of the rider now unnerved him as much as the tricks of the steed had done before, but the stranger thus attempted to encourage him. " Don't be frightened, but fasten in your nails. I am Donn Firinne, and am conducting ten thousand of my forces to wage battle and conflict against the fairies of Cork. My people are awaiting me outside your door at this moment."

All this was far from putting the village Vulcan at his ease; but, better or worse, he got through the job some way. The version of the story accessible to us mentions the conclusion of the shoeing, the adjusting of the shod portion to the rest of the leg by Donn, the shouting of the tribe when they saw their chief emerging from the forge, and the speed with which they escaped from the blacksmith's sight. Donn seems to have been in such a hurry, that he omitted to make any compensation to the black artist for his trouble.

CLIONA OF MUNSTER.

CLIONA, the most powerful, and at the same time the most wayward of the Munster fairies was daughter of the terrible Red-haired Druid who once threw a thick darkness over a Northern force set in battle array against the Southern men, and thereby effected their defeat. *Cliona* and *Aoibhil (pron.* Evil*)*, were his daughters; and Caoimh the Pleasant (O'Keeffe), a neighbouring chief, was suitor for the hand of the younger (Evil). Cliona happening to have her affections set on Caoimh, brought a wasting sickness on her sister, and at last the appearance of death, by the administration of a narcotic. She was interred, but the spiteful Cliona had her conveyed to a cave at Castlecor, where, under the appearance of a cat, she is still occasionally seen. Her other quarters are at Carriglea, near Killaloe.

Cliona's Court is five miles south of Mallow, in a lonely district: it consists of a rock in the centre of a circular space, surrounded by other smaller ones, the whole enclosure (about two acres) carpeted by the finest turf, and no rocks interrupting the view for a considerable distance. Belated travellers have seen Cliona and her troops holding consultation here, or leading the dance round the delightful enclosure. On winter nights frightful noises have been heard from Carrig Cliona, and no peasant or peasantess would enter or cross the eirie place after nightfall for any consideration.

As Cliona was once disporting in the neighbourhood by moonlight, under the appearance of a white rabbit, she was espied and made captive by an unlucky farmer, who bore her home, and kept her well secured. From the moment of her unwilling entrance into the house misfortunes descended in a storm upon the owner. Floods carried away his stacks, his cattle were missing, and at last two of his children lay on the bed of death. Within the space of a week all were at their wit's end, till some one remarked on the presence of the rabbit, and the beginning of their woes as occurring on the same day. The hint was sufficient.

The unlucky animal was liberated, and the children recovered. The strayed animals were found, ill-luck left the place, and white rabbits were carefully avoided for the future by every member of the family.

There was a "hurling" in the glen by the side of the river Feale, and among the spectators were James Roche and his son John, a child of seven years old. Cliona came out of the rock, unseen by any one in the crowd, and throwing a cloak over the boy, she led him into her cavern, and for fourteen years he was never seen by mortal. At the end of that period he presented himself to the eyes of his father, a full-grown young man, and while fear and joy were struggling in the heart of the old man, he thus spoke: "Dear father, I have been kept by Cliona in her rock for fourteen years, and now she is obliged to let me be seen by my family. If you cannot free me from her power in three months, she will oblige me to marry a young woman whom she stole when a child, and neither she nor I will ever again enjoy the society of our kind. If you travel to the lower part of Ireland, and persuade Kathleen Dhu, who lives by the church of Clogher, to come with you, she can free me from the enchantment in which I am held."

It was not long till the sorrowful father was on his journey, and after long travelling and much fatigue he was in the presence of the dark witch. She was ill of a fever at the time, but told him her daughter was equally powerful with herself, and would return with him if he would liberally reward her. "There's nothing in my possession she may ask," said he, "that I can refuse, if she free my son from the Sighe."

So they set out, and in due time they arrived at his house. "Get me now," said she, "the skin of a newly-killed sheep." It was got, and dried, and the wool plucked off, and she put it on as a cloak with the flesh side out; and so she and Roche presented themselves at the entrance of Carrig Cliona. "Hail Cliona of the Carrig!" said she. "A long distance I came to see you, all along from the church of Clogher, *where the birds speak to the border of the foxes.* If John, son of James, has wedded the young woman of the Sighe, or kissed her lips, woe and wrath shall light on him, and her, and on their mistress, Cliona, daughter of the Red Druid."

At these threatening words Cliona came forth, and was dismayed by the long coarse hair of the young witch that fell to her hips, and by the cloak of raw hide, with horns, legs, and all hanging about her. She had put a druidic charm on her eyes, that even made the Sighe tremble. "Who are you?" said she. "Are you Aoine, or Aoibhil of the Gray Rocks, or Ana Cleir, come hither from Bemus, or a witch westward from Beara?"

"No, I am not of your race at all. I am of the Bollar Beamish, and my brother is *Slawbocht no Treamhie* and the *Ruiddhera Rua*, (Red Knight), from the harbour of *Ben Hedir* (Howth). My other brother is *Dorrin Deidh gal*, who can make the old young, and the young old, and raise the dead out of the earth, and the Ard Righ of the *Sliochd Sighe* of Erinn has given me the run of all the country, and if I meet with refusal or evil treatment, he will come and take sharp revenge for it."

Cliona was overawed by the wild appearance and the threatening language of the daughter of Black Catherine, and she gave up John, son of James, praying that the witch might be nothing the better for her acquisition. But she was the better, for when she flung off her raw cloak, and her long head-covering of coarse horsehair, and stood before John, son of James, as a dark-eyed, beautiful young woman, he said if she would not become his wife he would return again to the Sighe of Cliona. The father gave his consent, a little unwillingly; but our authority has afforded us no information on the subject of the subsequent housekeeping of the young couple.

A loud noise as from the surging of a wave is occasionally heard in the harbour of Glandore, county of Cork, both in calm and stormy weather. It is the forerunner of the shifting of the wind to the north-east. It is called the "Tonn Cliona," or Cliona's wave, and was supposed in days gone by to portend the death of a king or great chief.

The much-lamented scholar and estimable man, Mr. John Windele of Cork, furnished the editor of this work with the following bizarre tradition:—

A BULLOCK CHANGELING.

IN the famed kingdom of Kerry, and not far from Tralee, stood the estate of Mr. Bateman, who, among other valuable cattle, owned one fine bullock, not to be matched in the seven neighbouring townlands for size and condition. But all at once he unaccountably began to fall away, and at last might be exhibited as a bovine living skeleton. All attempts to put fat on his unfortunate ribs by oil or other cake were fruitless, and at last Mr. Bateman gave him to one of his tenants to convert him to any use he pleased. He, knowing the folly of attempting to turn him to profit while living, imagined his death instead, and sold him to a Tralee butcher for little more than the value of his hide. The honest flesher, wishing to realise at once, put his prize in a suitable knocking-down position in his slaughter-house, and, swinging his pole-axe, came down with a mighty blow where he expected to find his head. But the selfish animal, at the moment the axe cut deep into the floor, was cleaving the half door in good style, preparatory to a headlong charge down the street. The battle-axe man, not willing to be a loser, swept after him fully armed; and the neighbours, excited by his cries, and the pace of the ill-favoured ox, joined in the pursuit. He kept his odds well; and when he came to the open gate of the demesne, he dashed through, and galloped direct for the old *lios*. Onward came in hot haste men, and boys, and dogs, but the more haste they made to come up, the less he seemed disposed to allow them. He scampered furiously round the fort, and by the time his pursuers arrived, hot and tired, no bullock was to be seen. While they were searching and wondering, the genuine and original ox was seen to walk out from behind a large bush, showing not the least inclination for a game at "fox and hounds." This was one of the few instances of an animal's being *bona fide* restored, and without injury.

HOW JOHN HACKETT WON THE FRENCH PRINCESS.

JOHN HACKETT was a Munster outlaw, one of the many who were put to their shifts after some of the old wars. He was travelling towards Holy Cross when darkness came on, and so he was benighted on the hill of Killoch, and debating with himself how he should pass the night. Meanwhile he held on walking about to keep up some heat in his body, when on a sudden he heard the sounds as of a company of horse galloping towards him from the north, but the noise they made only resembled the muffled sound of a whisper. When they arrived within a few yards of him, their chief cried out, "A steed and lance for John Hackett. John, you have to come with us." "Where to, sir?" "I am the chief of the Sighes of Ely," said he, "and am going straight to Paris to bring the daughter of the King of France home with me. I cannot do it, however, without human help, and you are my man. There is your steed; here is your lance; mount!" "With all my heart," said John, "but I must visit Dublin on our way, and the palace of the king of England when we are coming back." "That will be a great delay, but if it is necessary, be it so."

John bestrode the steed, took the lance in his hand, and in a few minutes they were at the door of his brother in Dublin. He entered but would not stop to eat or drink. He asked for a piece of parchment, ink, and a pen, and he wrote out these words, "I grant my Royal pardon to John Hackett of Munster."

He then joined his friends on the outside with his parchment, his pen, and his inkhorn, carefully secured in his clothes. They mounted their steeds, and as the next night was beginning to close in, they were standing outside the French King's palace.

They had made John invisible even as themselves, and all went in, and passed through the guests, and took their stations on mantel-pieces, and the backs of chairs, and looked on at the dancing. The princess was sitting by her father, and playing with a little spaniel, and enjoying the sight of the dancing. "There is my bride elect," said the fairy chief, "but I have no power while that spaniel is about her. Secure him, John; it is for that I brought you here." John went behind the royal chair, stooped, reached over his hand, and put the spaniel in his pocket. The same moment three arrows were shot at the princess by the fairy chief. She sneezed three times, fainted, and was immediately placed on a steed and borne away. What appeared to be her dead body was left on the spot where she had fainted, while she and Hackett and the rest were flying over the sea to England.

When they came to the palace of the king, all the troop but John remained in the cellar to refresh themselves, but the princess continued still, without knowing what was going on about her. John passed into the King's bed-chamber, and walked up to his bed-side. "Hillo! ho! King of Saxonland!" said he, "awake!" "Who dares disturb me out of my sleep?" said the king. "It is I, John Hackett of Munster, who asks your royal pardon and protection." "My protection to you will be the axe of the executioner." "Then," said John, drawing his sword, "I must be under the necessity of cutting off your Majesty's head." "Oh, oh! that is another thing; open the door and tell my attendants to bring me pen, ink, and parchment." "And maybe, your majesty, the cord or the hatchet besides. Here are the materials, only waiting for your majesty's fingers."

His majesty signed his name; John took the paper and vanished, and after some slight refreshment in the cellar, all took horse for Ireland, and in due time landed on the same hill from which they had taken him.

"What am I to get now for my trouble?" said he. "We'll fill your hat and pockets with gold." "I must have the princess also." "Say you so! You know what our arrows can do." "And you know what this spaniel can do," said he, taking it out of his pocket with one hand, and laying hold on the sleeping lady with the other.

All uttered cries of fright, and in two seconds there was not one of them to be seen. The princess awoke, and it was long before she recovered from her sorrow to find herself in a strange land, and in company with a stranger. He soon conducted her to a comfortable shelter with his friends, till he got possession of his own lands, and when her first surprise and grief was over, she made him tell her all about the carrying off. This he did, and at the end she liked him better than at the beginning, and this day better than the day before; and it was not long until they were man and wife in his own house and on his own lands.

When their second child was born, John said he'd go to Paris and acquaint her parents; and after some talking over the matter she consented. She gave him a letter and her scarf which she wore the night she was carried away. They put him in confinement till trusty messengers were sent to Ireland, and when these returned with the princess and children there was great joy. John was made a great lord, and if they didn't live happy THAT WE MAY!

———>◆◆◆<———

When the housewife's daily cares are over, she may make doors and windows as fast as she pleases; but if she neglects to stick the reaping hook in the thatch, or if she does not loose the wheel-band, or tie the hand-reel with a rush, or neglects to pour out the water that washed the feet by the channel under the door, those treacherous allies of the fairies will let them in.

THE FAIRY-STRICKEN SERVANT.

A TRAVELLING woman once got lodging in a farmer's house, and was provided with a bed in the kitchen. The sluttish servant-maid went to sleep in the settle, and was soon snoring soundly. About midnight the strange woman heard a tapping at the door, and a ghostly voice crying through the key-hole, "Where are you, Feet-water?" "I am in the tub, where I oughtn't to be." "Hand-reel, where are you?" "Lying I am on the dresser." "Reaping-hook, where are you?" "Lying loose on the floor." "Wheel-band, where are you?" "Drawn tight round the rim I am." "Feet-water, reaping-hook, hand-reel, and wheel-band, let us in?"

In came three wild-looking women to spend part of the night in comfort; but the turf had been allowed to burn out, and the hearth was unswept and comfortless. Two of them sat down, while the third searched dresser and drawers for some food. But nothing was to be found except a crust which the lodger had left for the *good people* on a stool near her bed. She took it, and returned to the hearth, and the three made a meal on it. "Ah, the negligent quean!" said one, who seemed the worst disposed of the party: "I'll leave her something to remind her of her negligence, and the only thing that can cure her is a poultice of this bread, left out by that decent woman in the corner. Let us not leave a crumb behind us." After saying this, she lifted a bit of thread off the ground, and threw it at the sleeper in the settle, and soon after all the company went away. When they were going out, the traveller, keeping her eyes nearly closed, saw the most good-natured of the three look at herself, and drop a few crumbs on the floor. While the women stayed, there was a dull light through the room, but the moment they left, all was as dark as pitch.

In the morning, the moment the woman awoke, she got up, and gathered the crumbs, and put them up carefully in a bit of rag in her pocket. About three months afterwards, she stopped another night in the same house. She had scarcely sat down when the servant girl began to tell her of a great swelling in her leg, that hindered her from walking any distance, or standing up at all beyond a few minutes: "and it's on me," said she, "since the very night you were here last." "Well," said the other, "let that *larn* you to keep a sod of turf alive all night, and sweep up the hearth, and leave something to eat for the good people when you don't throw out the feet-water, and stick the reaping-hook in the thatch, and tie up the hand-reel, and slack the spinning-wheel. If you'll promise to be more careful, maybe ourselves can do something for you." "Oh, musha, do, and God bless you, and it's me that'll be careful about what you say from New Year's Day to New Year's Eve." So the woman made a poultice with some hot water and the dry crumbs, and put it to the girl's leg.

It was not a minute on when the skin cracked, and a whole skein of woollen thread worked itself out. You may be sure that she gave herself tidier habits afterwards, and that the wise woman was welcome to a comfortable bed and a good supper and breakfast whenever she passed that way.

THE FAIRY RATH OF CLONNAGOWAN.

IN the townland of Clonnagowan, Queen's County, stands a rath which, about forty years since, was studded with old thorn trees. A Mr. Kinsella, to whom this, with the surrounding lands, was leased, took it into his head that he would grub up these ugly trees, make firewood of them, and get a good crop of wheat out of the hitherto useless circle. He was warned by the neighbours that if he attempted to do so, the *good people* would make him suffer; for, time out of mind, one person or another had seen them dancing, and holding their night festivals among these old stunted thorns. Nothing could daunt him. He fell to work, and began to grub up one of the trees, and had removed the sods and earth round it when he was called off on some pressing business. He was not able to resume his labour in the rath that day; and so at night he retired to rest, with intent to be early at his task next morning.

About midnight he was wakened by some unusual noises; and on opening his eyes he found the room all illuminated, though the moon was not yet shining, nor was there an appearance of candle or lamp anywhere. By this light he could see a score of little fellows in green frocks and red caps, the latter shaped like the fox-glove bell or the old Irish *birredh*. They began to move round the bed, and point their fingers, and make frightful faces at him, half the company moving one way, just close by the bed, and the other half moving in the other direction, outside them. He almost lost his senses in consequence of the confusion of their movements, and the spiteful gestures they were making. He attempted to roar out once or twice, but could not utter a sound, and he could only look and become more and more stupified and frightened.

At last there was a pause, and the mischievous creatures scattered themselves over the room, and seizing on everything that came in their way, they piled them upon the poor man, till he thought that the weight of the whole house was crushing him; and so disturbed was his mind, that he fancied the bed was pressing him down as well as bearing him up; and the eyes of the little fellows were watching him through the legs of tables and chairs, and shooting icicles of fire and ice into his brain. Then, lest the weight should be too light, they would spring up on the heap of furniture, and jump and prance till he could feel the hard wood and iron piercing in between his ribs, and squeezing his stomach flat on his backbone, and almost crushing his bones to the marrow. He was not able afterwards to tell how relief came to him. When he awoke in the morning he found the different articles of furniture each occupying its own place; but his bones and muscles felt so sore and bruised that he could hardly stir them; and his skin was blue, and purple, and black. The first use he made of his tongue was to direct his sons to repair to the rath, and put the removed clay and sods into their places of yesterday morning. Perhaps it was owing to the subsidence of the anger of the *Duine Sighe*, on witnessing the reparation, that he speedily recovered from the effects of his bruises, and his skin resumed its natural hue. We are unable to say what appearance the rath now presents. Near this village of Clonnagowan is the farm-house of Clonnaquinn, the bawn of which lies directly in—

THE FAIRIES' PASS.

It is known that the hill-folk, in their nightly excursions, and in the visits of one tribe to another, go in a straight line, gliding as it were within a short distance of the ground; and if they meet any strange obstacles in their track, they bend their course above them or at one side, but always with much displeasure.

A farmer named Finglas, a stranger to the old ways of the country, took this farm, and was not at all satisfied with the accommodation offered by the old farm-house and yard.

There was neither cow-house nor stable, except an excuse for such conveniences at the end of the yard. He would have new buildings made at the side, and dug out the foundation at once; but was warned that the Fairies' Pass lay directly across the bawn, and that it would excite their sovereign displeasure to find stable, or barn, or cow-house in their way. Unhappily Finglas, though married to a Roman Catholic wife, was himself a benighted Presbyterian, and as such, a contemner of all reverence due to the Good People. But see the result of pretending to be wiser than your neighbours. Scarcely were the buildings thatched, and the cows and horses installed in their niches, when the wisdom of the old people became evident. One animal after another, without apparent cause, began to refuse its food, languished, and died. In vain was recourse made to the most skilful cattle-doctors. Their medicines proved naught, and fairy men or women would have nothing to do with the devoted beasts; they were on the Fairies' Path. Not until three-fourths of his cattle were slain by the elf-bolts was Finglas overruled, and at last persuaded to construct new buildings at the end of the bawn.

Accounts of Banshees being easily met with in the works of Croker, Keightley, Mrs. Hall, &c., the inquisitive are referred thereto for information—the only one we mean to produce being, so to say, historical.

THE BANSHEE OF THE O'BRIENS.

LADY FANSHAWE, whose husband was ambassador at the Spanish Court in the reigns of the Charleses, First and Second, has left an account of an individual spirit of this class, which was seen and heard by herself. Being on a visit at the house of Lady Honora O'Brien, and having one night retired to rest, she was awakened about one o'clock by a noise outside one of the windows. She arose, withdrew the curtains, and beheld, by the light of the moon, a female figure leaning in through the open casement. She was of a ghastly complexion, had long red hair, and was enveloped in a white gown. She uttered a couple of words in a loud strange tone, and then with a sigh, resembling the rushing of a wind, she disappeared. Her substance seemed of the consistence of dense air, and so awful was the effect produced on the lady that she fainted outright. Next day she related to the lady of the house what she had seen, and the news was received with no marks of surprise. "My cousin," said she, "whose ancestors owned this house, died at two o'clock this morning, and, as is the case with the rest of the family, the Banshee was heard wailing every night during his illness. The individual spirit who utters the *caoine* for this branch of the O'Briens, is supposed to be the ghost of a woman who was seduced and murdered in the garden of this very house by an ancestor of the gentleman who died this morning. He flung her body into the river under the window; so the voice and appearance of this wailer causes more terror than those of other spirits, with whose grief there is no blending of revenge."

On one occasion, when the Bean Sighe of the Knight of Kerry was heard announcing by her wail the approaching demise of the chief, the merchants of Dingle, forgetting their plebeian births and occupations, took it into their heads to get frightened, lest the wild sounds should bode the immediate departure of some of themselves. A native poet, however, re-assured them in this wise:—

> "At Dingle when the lament grew loud,
> Great fear fell on the thrifty merchants,
> But fear on their own account they need not;
> The Banshee wails not such as they."

TOM KIERNAN'S VISIT TO FRANCE.

THE above-named worthy was a servant boy who lived at Ballydonoghue, near Tarbert. Being belated in the neighbourhood of a so-called Danish fort, he heard considerable noise within, and, coming close to the fence, he spied in a comfortable nook at the other side a party which he always afterwards described as fairies or witches, but could not tell which. At the conclusion of some (to him) unintelligible ceremony, they pronounced the words *Bruckas tha ussa* one after the other, and shot off through the air in a S. E. direction. "A fine thing to be able to do," said Tom. "*Bruckas tha ussa*, if you go to that," and away he flew in their train. All were soon in a wine-cellar in the south of France drinking like kings or fishes. When they had nearly emptied the entire of the vessels, they repeated the same words as before, and all soared back to Ireland, leaving the goblets behind. Tom, however, brought away his, and next morning gave it up to his master, with a full account of the expedition.

Several years after, a French vessel anchored in Tarbert, and the owner was entertained at the house of Tom's master, who, to do honour to his guest, produced his finest articles in plate, and among the others the captured goblet. The guest stared hard, as well he might, at the vessel, and eagerly asked his host how it had come into his possession. He furnished the needful explanation as to its being given up to him by Tom, and Tom's legend of its acquisition, which he by no means credited. "You may give entire belief to his story," said the other, "for I remember distinctly the morning on which our wine-casks were found empty and this goblet missing. We were nearly ruined by that very drinking bout," said he, "and have scarcely yet recovered. Let me, if you please, see the face of your Monsieur Tom." This hero being introduced, the stranger gazed on him for nearly three minutes as on one whose like he should never see again. Before quitting the house, with his lost property in his possession, he slipped a louis d'or into Mr. Kiernan's palm, and told him how happy he should be to see him at his home in France, provided he made the visit in the way familiar to ordinary mortals.

THE LOVE PHILTRE.—A Fact.

NORA, a healthy, bouncing young country damsel, but no way gifted with beauty, registered a vow that she would be the wife of young Mr. Bligh, a "half sir," that lived near.

The young fellow always spoke civilly and good-naturedly to her, but after a year or two's acquaintance, Nora saw no immediate sign of her vow being accomplished. She held consultations with adepts in fairy and demon lore, and discovered that the liver of a cat thoroughly black, white paws excepted, was sovereign in the process of procuring a return of love. Aided by her sister and another woman, researches were made, the cat discovered, and slain, with accompaniments which we do not choose to particularize. The liver was then carefully taken out, broiled, and reduced to an impalpable powder.

In a day or two the gallant was passing by Nora's cottage, and seeing her at the bawn gate he " put the speak" on her. She, nothing loth, kept up the conversation, and after some further talk, asked might she take the liberty of requesting him to come in and take a cup of tea. He did not think the better of her prudence for making the demand, but felt he couldn't refuse without incivility. So he was set comfortably at table, and Nora soon filled his cup from a black teapot, which, in addition to some indifferent tea, contained a pinch of the philtre. The guest began the banquet with notions and intentions not very complimentary to his entertainer; but when he took up his hat to walk home, he was determined on setting her up as the mistress of his heart and house. It is in the nature of this magic potion, that if the dose is not repeated at intervals, the effect becomes weaker, and at length ceases altogether. Nora, aware of this, renewed the administration at every visit, till his infatuation became such that he announced to his family and relations his immediate marriage with the cabin girl. Vain were coaxings, threats, reasonings, etc.; and at last the eve of the wedding-day arrived. Paying a visit to his charmer that happy evening, they were enjoying the most interesting and delightful conversation, when the latch was raised, and a party of seven or eight young fellows, armed with good hazel rods, entered and began to lay thousands on his devoted back and shoulders. Nora flung herself between, and received a few slight blows; but before they ceased practising on the amorous youth, every bone in his body was sore, and he himself unable to use arms or legs.

That was what they wanted. They trundled him into a car, and took him home, where he was tended and watched for a month. The drug not being administered all that time, he was amazed when he was able to quit his bed that he should ever have been guilty of such an absurdity. So to Nora's remorse for the unholy proceeding was now added chagrin at her want of success.

It is probable that *some* of the fairy fictions were the manufacture of scape-graces, who, to cover their neglect on certain occasions, got themselves out of disgrace by the invention of some wild adventures that had befallen them. An instance occurred to our own knowledge of a little boy, who, being sent for a pitcher of water at noon, did not return till past sunset, and then saved himself from discipline by a recital of a most dangerous ride on the back of the pooka, who had got between his legs while he was filling his jug.

THE POOKA OF BALTRACY.

YOUNG Pat Davidson of this townland was sent by his grandmother for a pitcher of water about one o'clock in the afternoon, but it was not till sunset that the truant, whose absence had caused great disquietude in the interim, was seen coming up the meadow from the side of the wood where the well lay. He seemed much fatigued, and various rents were visible in his clothes, and scratches on his naked legs. His overjoyed grandmother went down the path to meet him, but she took good care to dissemble her feelings. She looked at him with lowering brows, winding the strings of her *praskeen* [apron] the while round that useful article, presently to do the duty of a whip. "You *villian* o' the world!" was her first greeting, "what kep' you till now ? where were you loitering ?" "Oh, granny honey, it's well you ever seen me again! look at me clothes, an' me poor legs!" "Why, child, what happened you ?" "Musha, an' wasn't it the Pooka happened me: the curse o' Cromwell on him! Just as I was stoopin' down at the well to fill the jug, what did I see but his ears and his neck comin' out betune me legs, and before I had time to bless meself, off he was with me through the wood, knockin' me head again' the boughs, an' tearin' me legs again' the brush till we got through, an' were out in the fields. Oh, granny, such *sponshees* as he made over ditches and rivers, and so 'fraid as I was that I'd be thrown every moment! Well, at last, where were we chargin' but at the house where aunt Bessy lived, *and that the roof is off* [whose roof is off]. He run full plump up to it, and when I was expectin' to have me head broke again' the wall, there we wor thro' the winda, and never crack cried till we got to Cloncurry. Well, there he put his ugly nose to the ground, and kicked up his *hine* legs, thinkin' to have me down in less than no time, but I held to the mane like vengeance, an' gripped his sides wud me knees. He turned back there and give me the same *keerhaulin'* till we got to the well again, and then he pitched me off like a sack of whate; an', granny honey, isn't it a mercy that you ever seen me again?" "Oh musha, my poor paustha [child, *pais*], but it's grateful I am that the divel of a pooka wasn't allowed to murdher you. Come in alanna!" etc.

The winged words of this story soon went through the townland, and when Pat presented himself at school next day the faithless master began to question the hero on the particulars of his ride. The youth, either discomposed by the cold glances of the judge's eyes, or rendered by the terror accompanying the exploit incapable of exact recollection, was found to vary from himself in some essential particulars, and the result was a severe *hoising*. After some time, when the wounds were ceasing to smart, and the master's back was turned, an urchin had the ill nature to jeer him for telling such a bare-faced lie to his grandmother about the pooka. "Oh the *sarra* pooka you," said he, "if you were there, an' saw granny lookin' so vicious, an' twistin' her *praskeen* to leather you, you'd invent a worse thing yourself."

The ensuing legends cannot in strictness be classed under our general title, as they possess only local interest. However, there are none among them which are not popular in some part of the country, and therefore they are considered worthy of a place in our collection.

THE ENCHANTED CAT OF BANTRY.

LONG ago, after the English first came to Ireland, there were continual fights and skrimmages between themselves (their great strength was down in the baronies of Forth and Bargy), and the people in the upper part of the country, who would have no rulers except the old royal blood of Leinster, the O'Cavanaghs. Parties from each side would drive away cattle from their enemy, and kill the owners if they resisted. A little bodach of the English side that lived off towards Ballinvegga came in the dead of the night with a boy of his to a lonesome house somewhere near the *Glounthaan*, killed the poor owner and some of his family, and drove away all the cattle that were in the place, and that was only a cow and a sheep. But mind, when they were getting home they found themselves pursued, and had no way to save their lives but by breaking into a chapel. I don't know whether it was the one at Rathgarogue or Temple Udigan.

When the crowd went by, and they were relieved of their fright, they began to feel hungry. So they killed the sheep, and were roasting a quarter of it at a fire they made out of old coffin boards, when a big cat with blazing eyes came in through the wall, and miawed out, "*Shone feol!*" [*Is uaim feoil*, flesh is from me, *i.e.* I want flesh]. They were so frightened they gave him the quarter that was roasting. When he ate it he licked his chops and roared out again, "*Shone feol!*" and so on till he gobbled up all the sheep and three quarters of the cow. Hoping that he'd leave them a bit for themselves, they were boiling a piece of the beef over the fire in the cow's hide, stuck up on four stakes with some water in the hollow, but he bawled out more vicious than ever, when all the rest was down the red lane, "*Shone feol!*"

Well, they gave him the piece that was simmering, and while he was *aten* it they got out and were making the road home as fast as they could. They were not a quarter of a mile away when the moon happening to show her face, the bodach's boy cried out, "Master, master, the cat is sitting on the crupper behind you." He turned round and was so wild with fright and anger, that he pushed at the tormentor with his pike over his left shoulder, and whether he was killed or not, down to the ground he came. *Ovoch!* in a moment you'd think all the cats from Blackstairs to Carrigbyrne were round them, and before they could look round, the boy and his horse were down, and the wild creatures tearing them limb from limb. The master set spurs to his horse while they were at their work, and never cried crack till he was inside his own bawn and the gate locked. He was more dead than alive when he got in, and couldn't tell what happened him for ever so long. At last he began to give his wife an account of what happened, but when he came to the blow he made with the pike and the tumble of the cat, a *kittlen* only half a year old that was sitting on a boss screamed out, "Oh, you thief did you kill my uncle?" and without another word she flew at his throat, and tore out a piece the size of her own head. If he hadn't gone on a murdering business, his wife wouldn't be a widow from that day to the last one of her life.

Visitors to the Devil's Glen are so occupied with its savage beauties, that they rarely give themselves the trouble of inquiring how the rough defile came to be so called. Father Domenech obtained the following legend on the subject in his sojourn among the Wicklow hills.

HOW THE DEVIL'S GLEN GOT ITS NAME.

LONG ago the deep and rugged glen was merely a long low hill, with many trees scattered over its surface. In its neighbourhood was a convent, the ladies of which, especially the novices, would enjoy the free air under the shades of these trees; and to the extreme annoyance of many young princes and chiefs, the lovely Aoife, daughter of a neighbouring magnate, entered the convent as a postulant for the veil. Young aspirants to the hand of the insensible princess came from near and far, to endeavour to shake her resolution. The rules of the convent not being strict, it was not difficult to gain sight and hearing of the princess, but every suitor left the house with a civil and decided refusal.

Among the crowd of REJECTED who occasionally sauntered in company under the trees on the slope of the neighbouring hill, and administered such consolation to each other as they could afford, was an ardent young prince, whose voice joined in most musically with the united chorus of the praisers of the fair recluse. Being frequently annoyed by the mocking expression on the countenance of a dark-visaged man among the suitors, when the rest were loudest in their eulogies, he at last civilly asked him did not the princess deserve even warmer encomiums than what she had as yet received. "There is no woman in Erin," said he, "who would not be won from what she considers right conduct, by manly beauty or profuse riches." "Princess Aoife would be proof to both," said the youth. "Be at the entrance of the convent to-morrow at noon, and I will convince you of your mistake. She shall be subjected to the influence of beauty to-morrow; if that fails, gold shall be tried next day."

As the prince was sitting sadly enough on a stone before the gate at the hour appointed, he heard the sound of horns executing an enchanting melody, and beheld a mounted chief approaching, from whose jewel-covered dress light flashed at every step of his steed. His face and form were those of a beautiful and well-formed youth, and his retinue wore the most costly clothing. As he passed the prince, he said to him in the tones of his yesterday's acquaintance, "I am going to try the constancy of your adored princess. If you choose, you may enter among my train."

The prince endeavoured to shout "treachery" at the top of his voice, but an attendant touched him with a wand which left him powerless to move or speak. There he remained till the glittering youth came out again, rather humbled this time. "Beauty has failed for once," said he. "Gold must exert its power to-morrow." When the train had passed out of sight, the prince recovered his faculties.

At a high point on the hill was an old stone cross, and

near it was the issue of a spring, but the neighbourhood was marshy, and the course of the little brook scarcely discernible with flaggers, and rushes, and shrubs encumbering the banks. As the prince mournfully sat and ruminated at the foot of the old cross, he at last fell asleep. During his slumber a beautiful form clothed in white flowing robes, and her long hair encircled by a wreath of shamrocks, appeared to him, "I am the Sighe," said she, "to whom the care of this stream is intrusted, and I wish that it should dance and sparkle in the sunshine, and that the sounds of its ripples and falls should come to the ears of man and woman. You can accomplish this for me, and punish the demon who seeks to turn Aoife from her duty by———" What followed seemed to be felt by his inward thoughts without meeting his ears.

Next day, as he sat on the stone, there came by the handsome and richly-clad youth, with slaves and horses laden with gold and precious stones, and behind and beside the treasures the same richly-dressed train which had been in attendance the day before. This time the prince entered to witness the conference. The gold, and diamonds, and pearls had no more effect on the right-minded Aoife than the supernatural beauty of the wooer. He begged and prayed, but in vain, and he fell into such agitation, that his tail escaped from under his sparkling tunic, and began to lash about him in fury. This was what the prince was waiting for. He flung his praying chaplet round it, and the demon gave such a spring as took him out over the court, and on to the green hill-side. He sped to the spring, but the shade of the stone cross was on it, and he dared not come near. Overcome by the power of the sacred talisman, he flung himself down, and rolled about in agony, tearing away the soil and stones, and flinging them far on each side.

Thus he burned, and tore up, and flung out earth and rocks for the entire length of the present glen, when the prince, seeing no further impediment to the free course of the stream, relieved him of the torturing beads. When released, he turned on his tormentor to tear him to pieces, but a glance at the chaplet sent him through the air fleeter than the stone hurled from a sling.

The fairy had now the joy of seeing her stream soon increased to a goodly river, leaping from ledge to pool, and rejoicing in its course in the free air and sunshine.

If the prince did not persuade Aoife to be his bride, she induced him to become a monk in the neighbouring monastery. When God *really* calls, it is sinful not to obey.

One of the most beautiful of the Ossianic legends relates the carrying away of the poet to Tir-na-n-Og out under the waters of the Atlantic, his return to the earth after a century had elapsed, and the loss of his strength and manly beauty on his touching the earth. All this shall be told in our succeeding volume. Meanwhile we proceed to show the connection which our story-tellers established between our national saint, our national poet, and Cashel Cathedral, though St. Patrick never superintended the laying on of one row of its stones, and Oisin was in his grave about a century and a half before the holy man commenced his labours. The building stands on an isolated rock in a plain, and if our peculiar authorities are to be relied on, that large mass of stone was bitten out of a mountain westward by the devil in one of his fits of evil temper. Flying away with it between his teeth, he was obliged by some holy personage to drop it into its present position, to be a stance for the future sacred building.

THE ROCK OF CASHEL.

WHEN St. Patrick was building the great church on the Rock of Cashel, the workmen used to be terribly annoyed, for whatever they put up by day was always found knocked down next morning. So one man watched and another man watched, but about one o'clock in the night every watcher fell asleep as sure as the hearth-money. At last St. Patrick himself sat up, and just as the clock struck one, what did he see but a terrible bull, with fire flashing from his nostrils, charging full drive up the hill, and pucking down every stone, stick, and bit of mortar that was put together the day before. "Oh, ho!" says the Saint, "I'll soon find one that will settle you, my brave bull." Now, who was this but Usheen (Oisin) that St. Patrick was striving to make a good Christian. Usheen was a very crooked disciple. When he was listening to pious reading or talk, his thoughts would be among the hunters and warriors of his youth, but he loved the good Saint for his charity to himself. The day after St. Patrick saw the bull, he up and told Usheen all about what was going on. "Put me on a rock or in a tree," says Usheen, "just by the way the bull ran, and we'll see what we can do." So in the evening he was settled comfortably in the bough of a tree on the hillside, and when the bull was firing away up the steep like a thunderbolt, and was nearly under him, he dropped down on his back, took a horn in each hand, tore him asunder, and dashed one of the sides so hard against the face of the wall, that it may be seen there this day, hardened into stone. There was no further stoppage of the work; and in gratitude they cut out the effigy of Usheen riding on his pony, and it may be seen inside the old ruins this very day.

I think the black fellow did not covet a second visit from Usheen.

A person pretending to have been on the rock, says there is a rude mark, as of the side of an ox, on the outside of one of the walls, and a knight mounted on a diminutive quadruped in bas-relief within.

THE TREE OF THE SEVEN THORNS ON THE CURRAGH.

DURING the great plague and famine of 1439, there lived in a castle near this hill one of the powerful O'Kellys. He had several sons, of whom Ulick was his chief favourite. The father was a hard-hearted, proud, and selfish man, and the handsome Ulick was a compound of pride and licentiousness. He had brought many young women to ruin without scruple or remorse. Among these was the beautiful and graceful Oonah More, whose lot was not so very wretched, as she sincerely repented of her sin, and devoted her remaining life to the solace and relief of the poor creatures attacked by the pestilence. Her brothers, who tenderly loved her, and were keenly alive to the disgrace inflicted on the family honour, were on the point of seeking out the betrayer and putting him to death, when they heard that Providence had anticipated them. Ulick was seized with the pestilence, and in spite of his wretched father's remonstrances and prayers, removed in his bed to the side of a field fence by his brothers. A shed was fixed over him to keep out the rain and the sun, and a pitcher of water and a griddle cake, marked with a cross, were left by his side.

Oonah heard of his pitiful state, and whether her Christian compassion was influenced by former feelings or not, she came to his bedside, administered all the solace in her power, and supplied every little convenience that might alleviate his sufferings. Before her coming, his cries and complaints were heard fields away, but from her first visit no groans nor cries escaped him but such as were wrung from him by excessive torture. For days and days she attended on him, and succeeded, let us hope, in awakening his soul to the sense of his past guilt, and the necessity of true contrition.

One day the poor girl was observed sitting motionless, with her face turned towards the bed. *Scaldcrows* were flying about the shed and attempting to enter it, but were continually driven away by a milk-white bird. When a couple of days had gone by, and she was still seen in the same position, and the carrion crows attempting to enter under the shed, and the white bird still driving them away, the neighbours drew near and called to her to come home. But her soul had gone to its home in heaven.

They placed her body beside that of the repentant sinner, they set fire to shed and all, and from the ashes sprung the "Tree of the Seven Thorns," which remained to modern times. On its branches a white bird was continually uttering melancholy notes, and never stirring from its perch at the approach of man or woman.

LEGEND OF THE LOVER'S LEAP, IN THE DARGLE.

MARY, a capricious damsel of this neighbourhood, showed some preference to one of her lovers named Edward, while she was really attached to another. The first displayed perhaps too much devotion to herself, and too much attention to her slightest wishes. One day she expressed a desire for a certain kind of necklace, and Edward said he would at once start to Dublin for it. She told him not to fatigue himself, and not to think of returning that day. He was too anxious to gratify his lady with the sight of the ornament, and to display his own zeal, to allow himself such indulgence. Late the same evening he was hurriedly pacing along the bank high over the Dargle towards her house, when on a mossy hillock he discovered her listening, with every sign of loving interest, to the discourse of the secretly favoured rival. He took out the necklace, laid it on the grass before the frightened false one, walked rapidly to the edge of the overhanging rock, and plunged down, smashing bushes and shrubs in his descent.

However the young girl afterwards employed herself, the dismal clang of the funeral bell of her destroyed lover never left her ears. She took an intense dislike to the man for whom she had deceived him, and by dint of ever dwelling on his tragic fate she became insane. She haunted the fatal spot, and at last, being under the strong delusion of seeing her lover beckoning to her from the opposite side of the ravine to come to him, she sprung from the fatal spot and perished. Her spirit is still seen on the eve of St. John traversing the fatal locality in the form of a milk-white fawn.

THE DISCOVERY OF MITCHELSTOWN CAVES.

Here is a legend which has already grown up round the Kingston caverns, discovered some thirty-five years since.

A POOR man, named Gorman, who laboured on the Kingston estate between Cahir and Mitchelstown, observed one day while quarrying, that, according as he loosed the stones they fell into an underground cavity. Scrambling down after them he became the discoverer of these caves, the finest yet discovered anywhere. So much for the groundwork; now for the embellishments. Gorman was a model of a lazy philosopher of the cottier class. One day, when he was pretending to be weeding his potato-plot, he heard the bleating of a sheep, but there was neither sheep nor grass within the field. Examining diligently around he came to an opening, and getting down through it he found a poor sheep suffering with a broken leg. He lifted her up carefully, brought her to his cabin, and was about making mutton of her; but she looked so pitifully in his face that he could not find it in his heart to draw her blood. His wife washed and tied up the limb, gave her provender, and the poor animal soon could use the leg. In time she had two lambs. The wool of the sheep and lambs resembled silk, and brought four times the price of ordinary wool; and in a reasonably short time their lazy master became a comfortable farmer.

The venerable great grandmother who had brought this luck into the family was grown old and useless, and it entered the head of the ungrateful Gorman to kill her for St. Martin's day. In vain his better dispositioned wife strove to dissuade him from the thankless act. Kill her he would next day. The morning came, and with it came the young herd to Gorman's bedside. "Get up, master," said he, "every sheep on the pasture has gone away, and not a *crubeen* of them can I find anywhere." Up he jumped and put on his clothes, and to the fields with him without saying a prayer, or even blessing himself. After a long chase he came up with the sheep and drove them home; but as they passed the hole from which he had taken the first of them, every one of them slipped into it, and he might as well have thought of catching last year's snow as gripping one of their fleeces. Down after them he went, but he found all empty, and when the neighbours joined him with dipped rushes and *fangles* [lighted cones of banded straw, the French *faineul*], and looked about, they found the beautiful caves with their alabaster pillars and ornaments. The sheep were lost for ever.

LORD CLANCARTY'S GHOST:
A LEGEND OF BLARNEY CASTLE.

A MODERN proprietor of Blarney Castle took the liberty of cutting down various old trees which had shed honour on the grounds for centuries. Having received the price of them in Cork, he returned home wet and weary, ate a hearty dinner in the "King of Sweden's room," warmed his inside with a couple of tumblers of hot punch, and with the feelings of a man who had done a good action, betook himself to his arm-chair to enjoy a sleep.

At midnight he awoke and rung for his body-servant, Thady, and immediately after, heard a heavy and stately step on the grand stair-case. Looking towards the door, he saw a gentleman enter in the costume of James II.'s Court, holding a gold-headed cane in his hand. He ceremoniously saluted the proprietor, advanced to the window, and sorrowfully contemplated the trunks of the fine old trees cumbering the ground.

After a while, the last Lord Clancarty (for it was his ghost) approached the frightened "sleeper awakened," looked down on him sadly and sternly, and pointed with his cane towards the dismal scene abroad. He then stamped on the floor and vanished. At the same moment the castle shook, the bells began ringing, and every piece of furniture in the room fell down. The poor man was covered up with a mass of articles, and there he lay till morning. Thady then entering, cried out for help. Help came, and with some trouble the servants disencumbered the body of the poor man; and, by a good deal to do, he was brought to consciousness, the ghost not intending his death. However, he never ate another dinner, nor slept another night in Blarney Castle.

From among local narratives of adventurers who brave the rage of guardian cats, and hounds, and serpents, in pursuit of buried treasures, we select one adventure which we have from oral authority.

THE TREASURE SEEKERS OF MAYNOOTH.

It is said that under the ruins of Maynooth Castle may be found a cave from which a subterraneous passage extends to the old church-yard of Borreheen, some three miles distant. Rich treasures are reported to lie within this cave; and some sixty years ago a dozen young men, one of whom was lately alive, and related the exploit to our informant, set to work to clear away the rubbish from the entrance of the cavern. They worked away for two nights, withdrawing every morning before the daylight should reveal their proceedings; and after unheard-of toil, sinking a shaft, and then burrowing horizontally, they effected an opening into the vault. Just as they were clearing away the last obstacle, they found a piece of an ancient candle of an unhealthy yellowish hue, and a few minutes later the breach was effected. A violent current of air then rushed forth and extinguished all their candles. It brought such a clayey sickly smell with it that they nearly fainted. They lighted the candles again, but they were again blown out on the instant. At this point of the proceeding, their sentinel, who kept watch on upper earth, announced the approach of light, and all agreed to separate till welcome darkness fell on the old castle again. One of the party, however, remained in the neighbourhood of their burrow, to do what he could in case of the mining operation being discovered. As ill-luck would have it, an unbribable follower of the Duke's came in his rambles through the ruins, and stumbled on the fresh clay and the passage. He made no delay in apprizing his master of the fact, and he at once set a sufficient number of hands at work, to fill up the aperture again. This was a great blow to the adventurers, who had been sure of getting at the hoard early in the ensuing night. A watch was kept for some time afterwards, to prevent any more tunnelling. The man who brought home the candle remained convinced in mind, that if they had lighted it they would have gained the spoil. He lighted it several times, and from the rate at which it burned he calculated that it would have held out for a week. This is a sufficiently flat tale of treasure-seeking, but in the writer's judgment it is true in all its main points.

THE ORIGIN OF LOCH ERNE.

At some early period of Irish history, the region now covered by this beautiful sheet of water was inhabited by very wicked people. They were supplied with water from a fine well sunk deep in the earth, and the upper part was surrounded by a handsome circular frame of stonework. A benevolent fairy king or queen had favoured the earlier inhabitants by the grant of this spring-well, and the only conditions were that they shonld never leave it uncovered. The descendants of these good people proved a wicked race; and after many years their destruction approached. As a woman who lived near the spring was filling her earthen vessel one evening, she heard her child, who had been left in the cradle, cry out pitifully. Forgetting the fairy's injunction, she snatched up her pitcher and ran home; and instant attention to the infant's wants, and afterwards some pressing household concerns, put all connected with the well out of her mind. Towards morning the inhabitants of the valley were awakened, one after the other, by the chilly plash of water rising round them as they lay on their beds. Many were unable to escape at the low doors, as the surface of the flood was already on a level with the lintels. All the children and aged people perished; and the legend does not inform us whether the few vigorous sinners who succeeded in effecting their escape reformed their lives or not. At the next rising of the sun his rays no longer fell on houses, and gardens, and fields, but flashed instead on the smooth surface of a long inland sea.

THE DEATH OF THE RED EARL.

The ruins of *Athassel* (Ath Caisiol, castle at the ford), stand where once flourished an extensive monastery. There was a subterranean passage which conducted from it to Castlepark on the other side of the Suir; and when the monastery was invested in the old troublous times, and the inmates obliged to have recourse to this means of escape, the most advanced of the fugitives were some distance on the east side of the river when the last were only quitting the building. At this point, the abbot, who was among the vanguard of the party, missed his richly-bound illuminated breviary. There was no occasion, however, for any one to return. The word was passed from front to rear, and in a few minutes, the book being searched out by the last man, was transferred from hand to hand till it reached its owner.

In time the building and its dependencies became the property of De Burgho, the Red Earl, who was about as tyrannical and as uncharitable a nobleman as ever trod on Irish soil. One day a poor creature accosted him at his gate, and begged for relief, as he was nearly perishing for hunger and thirst. He spoke harshly to the beggar, and bade him begone. "At any rate," said he, "allow the servants to give me a draught of milk." "No." "Well, water." "Not even water: the river is not far—go and drink as much as you like from it." "Ah, then, my lord, as great as you hold yourself now, it might happen that you may perish yet for want of a drink of cold water." The earl called his dogs, and set them on the poor man, but they could not be induced to worry him; and he saw by the faces of those about him that they were far from approving his harshness: so he turned into the courtyard.

Several years went by; and on a very warm summer evening the Earl found himself all at once very ill, and afflicted with a violent thirst. He stretched himself on his bed after some efforts to bear up against the attack, and requested a draught of wine. All the vessels in the beaufet were examined, and not a drop found. The servant thought that very strange, as he had seen abundance of it there just after dinner. "Go to the cellar," said the earl, "and be quick about it." The poor fellow soon returned with great fright on his features, but his flagon empty.

lay. If he was able he would have followed them with a whip; but his limbs were powerless, and he was suffering dreadful agony from excessive heat and thirst inside. "Go," said he, as well as he could, "and let me have even a drink of milk." Off went one or two more, but they were in no haste to return. At last one was hardy enough to put in his head and say, "Ah, my lord! the dairy vessels are empty, and not a drop can be got from the cows." He was now in the most extreme terror and rage, but after uttering the word "water" with the greatest pain and difficulty, he could not get out another syllable.

Several ran off at the moment to the Suir, which lay a short distance to the east of the castle; but when they came to the bank, the bed of the stream was as dry as the hearth where a fire has just been burning. Several had joined the party, and all were in wild confusion. They threw up their hands, they ejaculated, they prayed, they were at their wits' end. On a sudden they heard a noise like the murmuring of a river on the west side of the castle. Off they ran, and found a newly-made channel; but the sound of the rushing water gradually growing faint, ceased altogether, and they only caught a glimpse of the last shallow ripples making their escape down the slope when they reached the margin. Some rushed after the retreating treasure, but it was too speedy for them. Again they paused; and now the rush and gurgle were heard in the old channel. Back they sped to find it dry, and to get anew the sound of the flow from the west side. Half of the crowd returned to the other course, and they all heard the rush of the river somewhere between them. They ran, each in the direction of the other body, and now they filled their vessels with ease from the welcome stream. They raised a shout, and ran to the castle; as they entered they heard their joyful cries answered from the dairy, from the byres, and from the cellars. The dying man heard the joyful tumult rushing up the turret stairs, and as the earliest-arrived entered the chamber, they beheld the convulsed features of their master in the last agony. His looks were eager, and he made a feeble motion towards them with his arm; but before the bed was reached, the arm had dropped motionless, and his sufferings in this life were over.

NOTES AND ILLUSTRATIONS.

HAIRY ROUCHY; *p.* 3.

The *ch* in the surname of this heroine must get a guttural sound as in all Irish words where it occurs. c and G never get the soft sound which belongs to them in such English words as *rancid, gem,* &c. In the tying of the three smalls, her waist, her wrists, and her legs above the ancles were secured.

In several of the household narratives of Teuton and Celt there was a profusion of bloodshed, and very small regret for maiming or killing outright. Were our labours of a purely archæological nature, we should not spare our readers a single horror of the many with which this class of fireside traditions abound. But we prefer cultivating for our little selection a popularity among folk whose joys are many, and years few, and to whom even the rough Juvenal declared that the greatest reverence should be paid. Therefore let our critics forgive us for using some of our materials with reserve, and relating deeds of cutting, thrusting, and gashing "with a difference."

Some forms of this present tale are of a decidedly truculent character. There is a variety of it in Campbell's West Highland Tales under the title of *Maol a Chliobain*, and another in Dasent's Norse Tales, where the heroine is called *Tatterhood*.

The professional story-tellers delighted in verbal repetitions at different points of the story, nor did even the good Homer despise them. They afforded intervals of rest. Economy of space is essential to our design and therefore we cannot indulge in them. However, when these stories are read out for children it will be found advisable to give all these repetitions without stint. The *Mishé* of the heroine will remind scholars of the *Outis* [no one] of *Odysseus*.

A LEGEND OF CLEVER WOMEN; *p.* 9.

The original compiler of this tale probably intended to question the wisdom of folks who delight in working out simple ends by complicated and difficult processes, such as that of promoting the happiness of a country by getting five-eighths of its able-bodied men killed in battle, or by the ordinary hardships of warfare. It is found in German collections under the titles—*Kluge Else* [Clever Bessy], *Klugen Leute* [Clever People], and *Der Frieder und das Catherlieschen*. Campbell tells it in his "West Highland Tales" under the title *The Three Wise Men*, and in another form as *Sgire mo Chealag*, which may be interpreted "The Parish of my Darling;" it is also to be found in Gerald Griffin's Works. The Italian Tale, *Bardiello*, belongs to the same class.

THE TWELVE WILD GEESE, p. 14.

The grouping of the white snow, the black raven, and the red blood, was put in requisition at an early period of story-telling. It is found in the old Cymric tale of *Peredur*, the original of "Sir Percival of the Round Table," also in the old Irish tragic tale of "The Sons of Uisneach," from which MacPherson extracted *Darthula*. The German counterparts are *Die Zwölf Brüder* [The Twelve Brothers], *Brüderchen und Schwesterchen* [The Little Brother and Little Sister], *Die Sieben Raben* [The Seven Ravens], *Sneewittchen* [Snow-white], *Marienkind* [The God-child of the Blessed Virgin]. In Dasent's Norse Tales the story is called "The Twelve Wild Ducks." In some of these stories a part only of our story is preserved. Among the Wends, [*Wanderers*] a people of Gallicia, it is called *Die Pathenschaft der Heiligen Maria* [synonymous with *Marienkind*].

THE WONDERFUL CAKE; p. 19.

One good feature in the household tales of the Aryan peoples is the attention paid to the sayings and doings of the animal world. The characters of most of the individuals introduced are marked by gratitude, and their exertions in behalf of their humane friends cannot be surpassed for earnestness and energy. In the earliest shape of the stories, these were all divinities in disguise. The essence of the legends escaped the story-tellers in time, but they retained the form. Many a young person must have beeen disposed by the hearing of these tales to treat the birds and beasts about them with due tenderness. These remarks are not so applicable to the present piece of extravagance as to other specimens of fireside stories.

THE FALSE BRIDE; p. 21.

Such tales as we are engaged with, stood in their original form thoroughly distinct from each other: but in the lapse of generations a part of one would be joined to a portion of another to make a separate story. Perhaps in the whole collection of Aryan folk-lore there is not to be found thirty per cent of purely distinct plots. In the present small collection it is hoped that there will not be found many repetitions. The German varieties of the present tale are *Die Gänzemagd* [The Goose-Girl], *Brüderchen und Schwesterchen*, *Die Drei Männlein im Walde* [The Three Dwarfs in the Wood], *Die Weisse und die Schwarze Braut* [The Fair and the Dark Bride]. In Dasent's Collection it is called "Bushy Bride."

THE END OF THE WORLD; p. 25.

Many light and apparently useless seeds are carried by their downy wings to foreign fields, while the acorn drops at the foot of the oak. *Foxy Coxy* is or was a familiar acquaintance with the peasantry from Cape Clear to Ulmea at the very end of the Gulf of Bothnia, yet how few individual peasants ever heard of the grave works of Buckle or Malthus!

THE THREE GIFTS; *p.* 25.

The cudgelling scene in this story used to give as much pleasure to the younger portion of fireside audiences as the marriage of Pamela did to the Windsor folk, who heard her story from beginning to end at a smithy during successive nights. It is met with among the Hindoos (somewhat disguised) by the name of "The Jackal, the Brahmin, and his Seven Daughters;" in the Norse Tales as "The Boy that went to the North Wind;" and in Italy as "The Woodman." Gerald Griffin has also told the tale, and Crofton Croker has embalmed it in his "Hungry Hill."

THE UNLUCKY MESSENGER; *p.* 30.

The following apologue in motley belongs to the family of fiction which claims "I'll be wiser next time" as a member. It illustrates the folly of expecting good management from an incapable person, however judicious may be the instructions given to him. He follows the rule laid down for him without taking circumstances into account. The other moral inculcated is the same as that in the fable of the man, his son, and their ass. Under a grotesque exterior many a one of the household tales conveyed an excellent lesson of practical wisdom.

THE MAID IN THE COUNTRY UNDER GROUND; *p.* 33.

This is one of the many household tales in which grateful animals figure. Another good specimen is preserved in the "Legendary Fictions of the Irish Celts" under the title of "Jack and his Comrades." Shakspeare or his authority borrowed the idea of the Three Caskets from some early variety of the story. The sentient and speaking tree testifies to the nature-worship of the pagan times from which the greater portion, if not all, of these fictions have come down to us. The Continental versions are the German *Frau Holle, Die Zwei Brüder, Die Drei Männlein im Walde;* "The Girl at the Well," and "The Stepsisters" in the Norse collection. The ancient Irish believed that the abode of the blessed, *Tir na n-oge,* was within the earth; the Greeks and Romans had their subterranean elysium, and we find the idea preserved in this old fireside tale and in the *Three Crowns* in the "Legendary Fictions of the Irish Celts."

JACK THE CUNNING THIEF; *p.* 38.

The title of this tale is the worst feature in it. Unlike the greater portion of modern rogue literature, it is not calculated to urge young folk to a breach of the decalogue. The curious will find other versions of Jack in "The Master Thief" of the Norse collection, and in the "Shifty Lad" of Campbell's "West Highland Tales." It is also to be found in one of Gerald Griffin's stories.

THE GREEK PRINCESS AND THE YOUNG GARDENER; *p.* 47.

The name Greece is spelled in our vernacular *Greig,* hence the peculiarity of the name in this story. The editor has heard the country so named on more than two or three occasions near the Wexford mountains. He hopes to escape blame for allowing his fireside chronicler to send his characters dry-shod from Spain to Greece *vid* Morocco. He has heard few foreign countries mentioned at Bantry or Duffrey firesides, except France, Spain, Greece, Denmark, Norway, and *Moroco*. The phrase "Through them with the boy till he got into the stable," p. 51, is idiomatic for "The boy went through them," &c. In foreign versions of the story, the elder brothers kill the youngest as they are returning, and dispute about the princess when they arrive. But the fox revives his favourite, and the traitors are punished. In Russian collections the story goes by the title, "The Fire Bird and the Grey Wolf," and a variety of it is called the *Czarewitsch Ljubim's Adventures*. It also appears as *Mac Iain Direach* [Son of John the Upright] in the West Highland Tales.

The Giant and his Royal Servants; *p.* 56.

The pursuit in this tale forms part of the story of "The Three Crowns" in "The Legendary Fictions of the Irish Celts." The whole tale is the same in substance as the late Wm. Carleton's "Little house under the Hill," in which the rich comic power of the writer was displayed. The present editor found it easier to adopt the seriou tone of the story as orally received, than to rival the *vis comica* o the author of "The Poor Scholar." It is told in Russia under the name of *King Kojata*, in Poland as *Madey*, in Hungary as "*The Glass Hatchet*," and in Germany as *Der Trommler* [The Drummer]. In the Norse collection it is called "The Master Maid," and in the "West Highland Tales "The Battle of the Birds;" the versions more or less differing from each other.

The Lazy Beauty and her Aunts; *p.* 63.

In Grimm's collection this story is called *Die Drei Spinnerin*, and a portion of it is found in *Rumpelstiltschen*. The Italian tales "The Seven Slices of Bacon," and "Goatsface," bear a strong resemblance to it. In the Norse collection it is entitled "The Three Aunts." Mrs. Ellen Fitzsimon furnished Duffy's Fireside Magazine with a charming variety of it under the title of "The White Hen."

Gilla na Gruaga Donna; *p.* 67.

A version of this tale is told in Germany under the title of *Die drei Soldaten* [The Three Soldiers].

Shan an Omadhan; *p.* 71.

J. F. Campbell has preserved a version of this story in his most valuable collection, "The West Highland Tales" under the title, *Mac an Rusgaich* [Son of the Skinner]. It would appear that the Bodach was guilty of a solecism in the construction of his order. *Staidhear do chosaibh na gcaorach* would be "a path *for* the sheep's feet;" *Staidhear le cosaibh na gcaorach*, a path *with* the sheep's feet. For neglecting the trifling difference between the two expressions, Shan made him suffer. The *sheep's eye* in the Bodach's meaning was a look expressive of mutual intelligence, or of wishing for something. Shan understood it in the sense which served his own purpose.

The Princess in the Cat-skins ; *p.* 81.

This tale will be at once recognized as a variety of *Cinderella* in the French repertory. The German versions are called *Allerleirauh,* [Rough altogether] and *Ashenputtel* [Covered with Ashes]. In the Norse tales the heroine is " Kattie Wooden-cloak." Campbell calls her fairy friend *A'Chaora Biorach Ghlas* [The Sharp Grey Sheep]. The Italians have a variety under the title of "The She-Bear."

The Well at the World's End ; *p.* 87.

This story is a relative of The White Cat in the printed fairy tales, and of " The Water of Life" among the Germans. " The Sick Queen" in the West Highland Tales has a slight connexion with it.

The Poor Girl that became a Queen ; *p.* 91.

This is rather a lesson of conduct under a grotesque disguise than a mere household tale. The German version is called *Die Kluge Bauerntochter* [The Clever Peasant Girl].

The Grateful Beasts ; *p.* 95.

Stories of this class are abundant in the folk lore of every people. They give evidence of animal worship having been contemporary with their invention, and in their preservation they display the genial kindly feeling towards all created beings, prevailing among groups of country people met to relax after their daily labours. The Mongols tell a story similar to this and under the same title. The corresponding stories told in Russia are the *Czarewitsch* [Czar's son] *Ljubim,* "The Fire Bird and the Grey Wolf;" in Hungary, "The Grateful Animals" and *Pengo* ; in Italy, *Gagliuso,* [Puss in boots] and The Jewel in the Cock's Head ; in Germany, *Die Zwei Brüder* [The Two Brothers] ; in India, " The Woodman's Daughter ;" among the Wends, (N. E. Prussia), *Der Krieg des Wolfes und des Fuchses,* [The War between the Wolf and the Fox].

The Gilla Rua ; *p.* 98.

In Italian collections a near relation of this story is entitled *Signor Scarpacifico.* In the Norse Tales it figures as " Big Peter and Little Peter." In The West Highland Tales it is represented by " The Three Widows" and " The Poor and Rich Brother." In " Holland Tide," by Gerald Griffin, it is called " Owny and Owny na Peak." S. Lover contributed a variety of it to an early number of the "Dublin University Magazine," with the title "Big Fairly and Little Fairly." *Cahir na Goppal* [Charley of the horses] was a noted horse-stealer, who used the lower story in the ruined castle of Leix near Portarlington, for stables. See the chap-book entitled, "The Irish Rogues and Rapparees."

The Fellow in the Goatskin; *p.* 103.

The descents made by Hercules, and Theseus, and our hero into hell, are probably modifications of a myth that was current in Central Asia before the Pelasgi made their first settlement in Northern Greece. The correct style of the name is *Giolla na Chroiceann Gobhair*. The fireside chronicler overlooked the fact of the King of Dublin being a Dane himself, and as such, in no dread of an attack by his countrymen. In a Flemish tale, *Fourteen Man*, by whose side the Irish youth is a dwarf, also pays a visit to the infernal regions, and astonishes the natives not a little. In the Polish story of *Madey*, a fine young boy goes down to recover a parchment signed by his father. On his return he converts a dreadful miscreant by describing the peculiar punishment preparing for him. "Yellow Bellies," a favourite nickname for Wexfordians, was given to them (by their own account) by Queen Elizabeth, when with yellow silk scarfs round their bodies, they won a hurling match in her presence. The free-spoken woman, rapping out a mouthful of an oath, protested "These Yellow Bellies are the finest fellows I've ever seen."

The Haughty Princess; *p.* 114.

Modifications of this story are to be found in all popular collections. Shakespeare had an old English version in his mind when he began "The Taming of a Shrew." Probably Tobin looked for no higher authority than Shakespeare for the outline of his "Honeymoon." The conclusion of our tale resembles that of *Griselda*, which Chaucer borrowed from Boccaccio, who himself had borrowed it from the Norman Trouveres. These gay minstrels did not invent the plot any more than their imitators. They found it current in the oral literature of their day. In the collection of the Brothers Grimm, the domestic reformer is called *König Drosselbart* [King Thrushbeard or Throatbeard].

Doctor Cure-all; *p.* 116.

In the German collection this worthy is called *Doktor Allwissend* [Doctor Know-every-thing]. Moliere founded his comedy of *Le Médécin malgré lui* [The Doctor in spite of himself] on an early version of the present tale long current in France, and seized on by the Trouveres before him. In the Gallic form, a rustic, being compelled to prescribe for a princess, effects her cure, and rather to his own surprise. All the sick of the city crowd next day to the palace to be healed, and the king orders the unwilling practitioner to go into the large hall where all are assembled, and put them out of pain. He enters, makes a speech to the infirm crowd, and promises an immediate cure, but then the greatest sufferer must allow himself to be roasted for the general good. His ashes taken on water are to be the specific. However no one would acknowledge himself to be ill on such terms. They make their escape by twos and threes, every one declaring to the king as he passes out that he has been miraculously restored to health, thanks to the royal physician. Of course the learned man quickly ascends to the top of his profession.

THE WISE MEN OF GOTHAM; p. 119.

A locality in one of the eastern shires of England would seem to claim these sages among its notabilities, but every country, almost every district, has its Gotham, to whose inhabitants everything which combines silliness with gravity is attributed by their neighbours. Some years since a book made up of such exploits from Hindoo sources, and entitled "The Surprising Adventures of the Venerable Gooroo Simple and his Five Disciples," was published by Messrs. Trübner. They appear to have been selected from the *Hitopadesa* by Father Beschi, and translated into the Tamul language in the early part of last century for the use of pupils. Father Beschi was one of the most learned, benevolent, and successful of Indian missionaries. The Tamul is spoken in the southern part of the Peninsula. Two of Grimm's stories, *Der Gute Handel* [The Profitable Bargain] and *Hans im Gluck* [Jack in Luck], resemble our tale in some respects. The early story-tellers, in order to interest their audiences for the time, and flatter their self-esteem, would tell similar stories, laying the scene in a neighbouring locality, whose inhabitants laboured under the dislike or contempt of the listeners.

THE GOOD BOY AND THE ONE THAT ENVIED HIM; p. 122.

This and the next two tales, and "The Music of Heaven," are among the apologues selected from the current household fictions of ancient times, and read for the inhabitants of religious houses when at their meals, or introduced by preachers into their sermons. The Trouveres converted "The choice of Three Evils" into a rather unedifying story, by their mode of telling it. "The Good Boy, &c.," is the subject of Schiller's Poem of The Road to the Foundry, so beautifully illustrated by Retsch. Johannes a Voragine, Bishop of Genoa, in the latter half of the thirteenth century, embodied most of the moral legends to which he had access in his *Legenda Aurea* [Golden Legends]. No clergyman of our days would venture on reciting to his congregation many of those tales once considered rather edifying, or as the name *Legenda* imports, "Things useful to be read." "The Music of Heaven" has always appeared to us one of the finest, if not the very finest, of all the saintly legends. "The Birth and Baptism of St. Mogue" and "The Greedy Mason" are fair specimens of the use which our old storytellers made of incidents in the lives of the Irish saints. In our old pagan lore a wonderful cow cuts an imposing figure. The daily restoration of the slain and eaten animal was a household incident among the Norse gods of Asgard, the boar affording a supper to Odin and the other divinities, and enjoying buxom life the next day.

HOW DONN FIRINNE GOT HIS HORSE SHOD; p. 131.

This pagan story was too curious to be neglected by the tamperers with the lives of saints. So they feigned St. Eloi, the skilful worker in metals, to be much puffed up with pride of skill, and an angel thus curing him of his spiritual malady. Coming mounted to his forge, he fashioned a shoe, pulled a leg out of his steed, shod the hoof, put the limb back in its place, made the beast go through his paces as well as if no operation had been performed on him, and asked the saint could he do such a thing. Of course he could (in his own conceit), but when he tried the experiment on a steed of his own, and saw the life-blood gushing out, and the poor beast at the point of death, he humbly besought pardon for his presumption, and obtained it. The angel assumed his ethereal form, administered spiritual comfort, and then vanished.

CLIONA OF MUNSTER; *p.* 133.

For the legend of this powerful Fairy Queen, see the *Dublin University Magazine* for November, 1870, the outlines of the story having been taken from a MS. obligingly lent to the compiler by W. M. Hennessy, Esq., M.R.I.A. The legend of the Red Druid is intended for publication in the forthcoming "Bardic Stories of Ireland." Probably the threatening rhapsody dashed in Cliona's face by the handsome young witch was as little intelligible to her as it will prove to our readers. "The Birds speaking to the border of the Foxes" must have inflicted no small degree of fright on her. The wildly attired maiden had surely heard in some way the equivalent of *Omne ignotum pro terribile*. Cliona and our other fairy queens detained Irish youths in their Sighe palaces, as Calypso and Circe did the comely hero of the Odyssey, ages before their day.

THE FAIRY-STRICKEN SERVANT; *p.* 139.

There were probably stories current among the country folk of Italy and Greece in which the Lares and Penates, or their representatives, punished or rewarded domestics according as they showed themselves negligent and slovenly, or the reverse. These household gods and the corresponding divinities of other countries have survived to our own times as fairies, brownies, Shakespearian lubber-fiends, &c. The fragments of food and the drinks spared to the fairies continue the libations made by the ancient pagans to the gods. If reapers and mowers neglect to spare scraps from their open-air repasts, the fairies leave a curse on the spot, which afterwards produces the *feur gorthach* (hungry grass). Whoever inadvertently crosses the doomed strip of verdure, falls down and perishes in a short time from mere weakness, unless he is discovered and given some food and drink. Wm. Carleton treated this superstition in detail in one of his stories.

THE FAIRY RATH OF CLONNAGOWAN; *p.* 141.

This and the next legend have been communicated to us by an unimaginative lady, a native of the locality. *The Love Philtre*, p. 145, is from the MSS. of my lamented friend, John Windele of Cork.

The Enchanted Cat of Bantry; *p.* 149.

In the volume of the Transactions of the "Historical and Archæological Association of Ireland" for 1868, and at pages 187 *et seq.* this legend will be found at full length. Its appearance in print dates from the middle of the sixteenth century. William Baldwyn the writer, asserted that as he was spending a night in company with Master Ferrers, master of the revels to King Henry VIII., Master Willot his astronomer, and Master Streamer his divine, this latter related the story of the Cat as having been told him while on a visit in the county of Vvashford at the house of a churle of Fitzheries (Fitzharris). We are indebted for the legend to Robert Malcomson, Esq., in whose possession the unique old volume rests. The present writer has ventured to give an English explanation of the language of the cat, who, as is only reasonable to suppose, miawed in the native tongue, and was from the beginning of the tragedy bent on annoying the strangers. Non-Irish scholars will please pronounce *Is* in the explanation as if spelled *Iss*.

The *Glounthaun* is a hollow through which the road to New Ross runs. It is considered an eirie spot by the Bantry folk.

The Mitchelstown Caves; *p.* 156.

The sheep in this tale are distant relatives to the sea cattle on Dursey island, on the Munster coast. These suspecting evil designs on the part of their keeper, repaired to their native element, leaving stone effigies of themselves on the shore.

The Death of the Red Earl; *p.* 160.

Ath Caisiol would be better explained by "The Ford of (or near) the Castle," but for the name being applied to the building, not to the river-pass.

Any of our readers who wish for a closer acquaintance with foreign folk lore, may enjoy it, provided they understand German, by consulting the following authorities:—

For GERMAN STORIES reference may be made to the collection of the Brothers Grimm, of which an edition was published at Berlin in 1822, and another at Gottingen in 1843. There are many separate collections of German household tales, for mention of which we cannot afford space.

For HINDOO STORIES, Dr. Herman Brockhaus's selections from the *Amadeva Bhatta* of Cashmere, published at Leipzig, 1843, and "Old Deccan Days; Hindoo Fairy Legends current in Southern India," collected by Miss M. Frere, Murray, 1868; also, "Vikram and the Vampire," edited by the great traveller R. Burton, 1869. In this collection the stories are told by a Vampire to King Vickramaditya, who is carrying him from a burial ground to a magician, in order to convert him to a certain use. If the King happens to answer any question which the Vampire insidiously proposes to him at the end of each tale, the cunning fellow escapes from his wrapping cloth, and goes back to his place, and the King is obliged to return and imprison him again, and another tale follows. Professor Theodor Benfey published at Leipzig in 1859 a translation into German of the Hindoo Tales found in the *Hitopadesa* [Good Advice], and the *Panchatantra* [Five Books], under the title, *Panchatantra, Funf Bucher Indischen Fabeln, Märchen und Erzahlungen* [Five Books of Indian Fables, Tales, and Stories]. There is a French paraphase of these stories by M. Dubois; Paris, 1826.

For HUNGARIAN STORIES see Saal's collection, Vienna, 1820; Magyar Sagas and Stories by Johann Grafen Maylath; Stuttgart und Tubingen, 1837.

For ITALIAN STORIES,—The *Cento Novelle Antiche*, a mixture of Saracen, Hispano-Moorish, and Eastern tales, and of those told by the French Trouveres; Straparola's *Le Tredici Piacevolissime Notte* [The Thirteen Very Pleasant Nights], 74 in number, and first published at Venice in 1550; and the *Pentamerone* of Count J. B. Basile, of Torone, a Neapolitan poet, who flourished in the beginning of the seventeenth century. Basile's tales are related by a Moorish slave. In *Del Dialetto Napoletano*, of Galiane, 1789, and in *D'Afflitto Memorie degli Scrittori del Regno di Napoli* of Eustach, 1794, will be found information concerning the last named writer and his works.

For MONGOL TALES we give reference to a German version of Benjamin Bergmann's "Nomad Wanderings among the Kalmucs in 1802-1803," printed at Riga in 1804; as well as Lehmann's *Magazin der Litteratur des Auslandes* [Magazine of Foreign Literature], 1838. The frame-work is the same as that of Burton's "Vickram and the Vampire." A young Khan, for expiation of his sins, has to fetch the vampire *Ssidi Kür* from the burial ground, and every time he gives a wrong answer to the question proposed to him at the end of each tale, the vampire escapes, and the Khan's labour begins anew.

Of POLISH HOUSEHOLD TALES, K. W. Moncicki made a collection, and F. W. Lewestan published a German Version at Berlin in 1839.

The RUSSIAN FIRESIDE TALES were translated into German, and published at Leipzig with a preface by Jacobus Grimm in 1831. Johannes R. Vogel published another German version of them in Vienna, in 1841. The best collection in the original Russ is the *Nowosselje*. Moscow abounds in chap-books of the kind.

The best SCANDINAVIAN LEGENDS of the Fireside are Arndt's Selection, Berlin, 1842, and a collection in a poetical form made by Afzelius, entitled *Svenska Folk Visor*, [Swedish Folk Stories], and issued at Stockholm in 1814, 1816. A German edition of this with a preface by Ludwig Tieck was published in 1842 at Leipzig. The latest collection by Asbjornsen and Moë has been given to the English reading public by G. W. Dasent, under the title of "Norse Tales."

The WENDISH TALES were published under the title *Volkslieder der Wenden* [Folk-lore of the Wends], by Von Leopold Haupt and Joh. Ernst Schmaler, at Grimma, 1843.

GLOSSARY.

The correctly spelled Irish words are printed in Italics. In these the hard sounds are to be given to c and g, and the final vowels to be heard.

AOIFE : Eve, a woman's name.
AOIBHIL : all lovely.
BANACHT LATH : *beanachd leat*, a blessing with you.
BAWN (before explained) has its root in *bo*, cow, being the enclosure in which cattle were gathered in the old disturbed times.
BODACH (same root), originally meaning a grazier, has come to designate a churl, a purse-proud, ignorant person.
BODHER (*buidre* deafness, *bodhraim* I deafen) : annoyance. "Moidher" is another form of the word.
BOORAWN : a domestic utensil for carrying meal or corn—a tambourine enlarged, has the same root owing to its drum-like sound when struck.
BRISHE (*brisé*, a breach ; FR. briser, to break) : smash, debris.
BRESNA : *brosna*, a bundle of sticks or brushwood intended for fuel.
CASHEL (*cios* tribute, *ail* rock) : rock of tribute. Cashel was the ancient capital of Munster.
CANNAT : probably from *Ceannaidhe*, a dealer, peddler, such folk being considered the reverse of simple or upright. The "canny sugach" (jolly packman) was a welcome, though not much trusted, visitor at farm-houses.
CLIONA : beautiful.
CLONCURRY (*cluan* a pasture, *currach* a race-course or marsh) : the marshy meadow, or meadow in the marsh.
COORAMUCH (*coirm* or *cuirm* banquet, *cuirmeach* festive) : comfortably social.
COSHERING (*coshair* feast, bed) : living at a neighbour's expense.
CUGGERING (*cumhgairin*, I convoke ; *comhgair* rejoicing, convoking, convenience) : holding confidential conversation with some one.
DARGLE (*dair* oak, *geal* beautiful, *dorcha* dark). The reader may assume the meaning to be "fair oaks," or "fair-shade," the latter equivalent to the "Beltenebros," of Don Quixote's library.
GAUM (*gam* gazing about) : a gaping, dawdling fellow.
GOMULA (*gamaillé*) : a gowk, a simpleton.
GOOD PEOPLE : *duine matha*, the fairies, said by way of propitiation. Waverley students will recollect " the kind gallows of Crieff."
GOOGEEN (*ge* goose, *ceann* head, *gugaille* a talkative fellow) : a silly person, a goose-cap.
GORSOON : *garsun*, the French garçon, a boy.
HAGGARD (stackyard). Besides the Irish names before quoted, there is also *adgort* (*adag* a bundle of sheaves, *cuirth* a yard).

KIPPEEN : *ceipin*, a dibble or planting stick.

LEWD : *ludar*, awkward, clownish, ashamed.

MODDHEREEN RUA (*madha* or *madhradh* a dog, *ruadh* red) : a fox.

OMADHAWN, before explained, boasts the cognate word "moodan" in Hindustani.

OXTER, *Oscal* (*Uchd* the bosom, *staidheir* (pr. *stair*), a step, a path) : the armpit. The pass from the bosom.

PISHROGUES (*pishreog* or *pisheog*, witchcraft) : magic spells.

PRASKEEN : *praiscin*, an apron,

RAMPIKE (*reimshé* staff) : a young tree stripped of its boughs and bark.

SARRA (*sar* contempt, disdain) : misfortune. Country folk sometimes combine the idea with that of an evil spirit.

SRAUMOGES : *sram*, matter oozing from the eye-lids.

STURK (*sturrach* rugged, *stuirt* pride) : an obstinate, disobliging person.

STHRONSHUCH (*sthro*, prodigality ; *strogh* a rent) : a lazy good-for-nothing fellow.

SHUCHRAWN (*sugradh* mirth, diversion) : state of dissipation and hopelessness (in modern slang "being on the batter").

THUCKEEN (*thoigheach* loving, *thocha* love, *thoghadh*, chosen) : a pet expression for a young girl.

⁎ To Irish or corrupt words in the book not here explained, the writer begs to refer to the glossaries of the three books mentioned in the succeeding pages. A well-digested, most masterly, and useful work on the names of Irish localities is Mr. Joyce's "Origin and History of Irish Names of Places." Colonel James A. Robertson has done good duty by Scotland in the same line.

LEGENDARY FICTIONS OF THE IRISH CELTS.
By PATRICK KENNEDY.
Post 8vo., Cloth, Illustrations, 7s. 6d.
MACMILLAN & CO.

The Athenæum.

"As an author combining archæological learning with a sly grave humour, we commend Mr. Kennedy to the public, reminding the latter that to the scholar and historian, the real value of the book lies in its archæology. In the latter department the author has rendered great services. . . . His book will keep his name young as an admirable Irish story teller."

The Spectator.

"This is a very admirable selection of Irish Fairy Stories and Legends, fresh and full of the peculiar vivacity, and humour, and ideal beauty, of the true Celtic legend. . . . Mr. Kennedy has produced a beautiful and popular book."

The Dublin University Magazine.

"No writer ever came to his work armed with a shrewder and more philosophic discrimination, with imagination and humour so in harmony with his subject, or with a more racy and admirable gift of narration. . . . He approaches the most grotesque and extravagant of his Celtic stories with the veneration due to immense antiquity, and rude but undoubted national inspiration. In him we admire not only an admirable story teller, but a man of quiet and pleasant humour, and a sound and comprehensive scholar."

The Dublin Evening Mail.

"It would be unfair to Mr. Kennedy, to treat his work as merely an entertaining collection of home tales. That it is, and much more. It is a vivid picture of the ancient Celts in their interesting superstitions, customs, kindly sympathies, and simple piety; and much is due to the reverent hand of the painter, who has lent to it no false colour, but presented the stories in their truthful simplicity. This will make his work a classic — one to stand beside the best books of folklore. We consider that he has laid Irishmen of every creed and class under an obligation, by a work which will offend none, and please and instruct all. The purest taste has presided over the selection and narration of the stories."

The Limerick Chronicle.

"Since the publication of Crofton Croker's 'Legends' and Keightley's 'Fairy Mythology,' no such attractive work of folk-lore and household fiction has appeared as the present. When we compare it with the above works, however, we must decidedly give it the preference for the comprehensive variety and local interest of its multifarious fairy tales, ghost stories, witchcraft, sorcery, fetches, and diablerie of every kind. It will bring back to many of us the most pleasing reminiscences of our childhood. At the same time the author's repertory has been so well filled from all our archæological stores, that the more learned and fastidious reader will find something to attract his attention, and add to his stock of knowledge. The book is in short quite a gem in its way."

THE BANKS OF THE BORO.

BY THE SAME WRITER.
Foolscap Octavo; 2s. 6d. free by post.
DUBLIN: M'GLASHAN & GILL, AND P. KENNEDY.
LONDON: BURNS, OATES, AND CO.
EDINBURGH: JOHN MENZIES AND CO.

The Athenæum.

"Under the cover of the tale, the author pourtrays scenes and incidents in Irish life in a simple unpretending manner. . . . On the thread of the story are hung illustrations of Irish life, legends, morals, and poetry, which are the real staple of the book."

The Spectator.

"For the somewhat numerous class who like to look at nations through a microscope, and those who are seeking to understand better many curious phases of Irish thought and feeling, this volume will have considerable interest."

The Dublin Evening Mail.

"Mr. Kennedy's picturesque sketches are as green, sunny, and vivid as a bit of landscape from a true artist's pencil. The scenes are full of character and innocent humour. The feature most marked in his sketches is the *life* which animates every page. We ask no truer painter of the Irish character, in its simpler and tenderer aspects, than the author."

The Nation.

"Here is no exaggeration, no straining after effect, no outrageous caricatures of the people. Yet a great amount of mirth and oddity is to be found in the scenes, and the warmth and intensity of Irish feelings is well displayed. We are taken to the wake, the dancing school, the hurling match, and the harvest-home, where the wit and humour of the country-folk run on right merrily. The jokes and the songs are often exceedingly comic."

The Irish Times.

"As a delineator of the people and their manners, the writer is perhaps unrivalled. This present work is characterized by a quaint, sly humour, pungency, and raciness. It is as remarkable for originality, for truthfulness, and simple philosophy, as for its wealth of information concerning curious customs, local traditions, and social gatherings, which the writer attaches to an interesting narrative of quiet country life."

The Freeman's Journal.

"This little work rescues from oblivion the household stories, manners, and amusements of half a century since. The style is pure and as simple as the habits the writer describes. Not the least interesting in the collection are the songs and ballads of his youthful days."

The Irishman.

"In the BANKS OF THE BORO we become a guest at the fireside of the comfortable farmer, and a confidant of the gossip that flows in fluent streams round his bright hearth. Episodes—racy, rollicking, and genial, and ballads of the real national type, are strung together on a string of fiction, as country children string the wild flowers of the field."

The Kilkenny Moderator.

"We have here a tale racy of the Irish soil. All the scenes are clearly drawn from nature, and the characters are the living counterparts of personages photographed in the memory of the writer. They are here produced with life-like effect."

EVENINGS IN THE DUFFREY;

BY THE SAME WRITER.

Foolscap octavo; 2s. 6d. free by post.

DUBLIN: M'GLASHAN & GILL, AND P. KENNEDY.
LONDON: BURNS, OATES, & CO.
EDINBURGH: JOHN MENZIES & CO.

The Athenæum.

"Attentive readers of these *Evenings* will be delighted with the faithful pictures of rural life, and with the light which is thrown upon the customs of country homes in Ireland. . . . They will see that a graceful wit pervades the every-day conversation of the country-folk; that they have deep religious feeling, and even possess some knowledge of history. . . . The manners which Mr. Kennedy depicts have not become obsolete. Long may they prevail! for they are those of a simple, virtuous people. . . . Mr. Kennedy's present work gives the reader a vivid picture of living Irishmen and women."

The Month.

"The course of the narrative introduces us into many an Irish home, and gives us the details of their every day life. Love, simplicity, and a taste for the marvellous are all blended together just as they are in the lives of the peasantry, with a free interchange of wit and practical jokes. But in nothing is the writer more happy than in the thoroughly Catholic tone which he has unconsciously imparted to all the acts and feelings of his characters. In pourtraying the superstitions of country life, he shows how much of sprightly romance and poetry there is about them."

The Irish Times.

"Mr. Kennedy has depicted the social and domestic existence of his *dramatis personæ* with such realistic minuteness, that those who desire to know what Ireland, at least the county of Wexford, was some quarter of a century before the great famine, will find much to their purpose in this work. The legends are extremely interesting and well-told. The *Usurer's Ghost* and the *Young Prophet* are amongst the most powerful we have read. In a different vein the tragi-comedy of the *Three Geese* and the *Earl of Stairs' Son* are equally excellent."

The Scotsman.

"None of Mr. Kennedy's stories are of the rollicking order, but all are full of good humour, fun, or pathos. Several ballads also occur in the volume, and some of them are capital. The volume is one which probably conveys as good an idea as can be got of the life of the industrious farmers and agricultural population of Ireland."

The Nation.

"The author's tales and pictures recal and preserve the life and love of a peasantry at once loveable and loving, kindly, quaint, and contented. The indulgent landlord surrounded by his tenantry, patronising the sports of the peasantry, and reaping the reward of his kindliness and generosity in the undivided affection of the people, is the centre of a charming picture."

The Dublin Evening Mail.

"The remarkable simplicity of the tales, their quaintness and purity, will sustain the character Mr. Kennedy has won for himself in his former works. Without exaggeration or colouring he represents the simple life of his countrymen when quietly allowed to pursue their ordinary occupations."

www.ingramcontent.com/pod-product-compliance
Lightning Source LLC
Chambersburg PA
CBHW020244170426
43202CB00008B/225